My wants to be a footballer

By Canaan McDonald

Sign up to grab your free guide!!

Go here: https://eepurl.com/df_zbH

© 2015 Canaan McDonald

All Rights Reserved

CONTENTS

ACKNOWLEDGMENTS 1

INTRODUCTION 2

IN THE BEGINNING 4

MATCH DAY 8

A NEW SEASON 18

TRAINING FOR A NEW TEAM 25

DISTRICT TRIALS 30

PLAYING FOR THE DISTRICT TEAM 37

PRE-SEASON TRAINING 66

A DIFFICULT TIME 75

IT ALL STARTS AGAIN 85

ANOTHER TOURNAMENT, ANOTHER CHALLENGE 97

TRUSTING YOUR GRASSROOTS COACH 102

FULLY FIT AND INJURY FREE 112

THE PRO ACADEMY ROUTE VS THE NON-LEAGUE ROUTE 120

END OF AN ERA 144

CONCLUSION 173

ACKNOWLEDGMENTS

Dawn Livingston

Caroline O'Mard

Canaan McDonald

Keoni McDonald

Aaron McDonald

Marcia Brock

Thank you, to all of you who have helped me and encourage me. Love you all.

INTRODUCTION

From six years old, my son, Canaan, has loved football. I thought I loved football, but I've got nothing on him: he is dedicated, disciplined, and totally believes he can have a career in football. I wanted him to get the best coaching and training possible at grassroots level. But how do you do that? Whom do you trust? How do you know that the coach you are letting work with your kid is not ruining their development? Does a coach having all his FA badges guarantee that he's a good coach?

Now, these are the questions I was asking myself as a parent. I didn't have any contacts in football and I am not a professional ex-footballer; I am an ordinary dad who loves football. One of the things I loved about it was technical players who don't love the skills, the flair, and the dribbling. Here was my problem: how could I make sure my son was being developed technically?

As I write this book, my son is fifteen years old and he is a technically gifted player. As you follow me on this journey, you're going to be amazed and shocked at what I've seen and heard in youth football at grassroots level; from coaches yelling at under eights to fifteen-year-olds not being able to do a basic drill like dribbling in and out of the cones. Along the way, I have met some amazing coaches, coaches who are the heart and soul of grassroots football. It's one of my reasons for writing this book as I feel coaches at this level are often forgotten. No one remembers them, no one sees them struggling when funds have been cut, or the sacrifices they make, having to deal with abusive parents, terrible pitches, and poor facilities. But they do it because they love it, because they have a passion for it and they want to give back. Where's the recognition? Why are they not treated as if they're important?

I'm going to give you the story of my son's development and, hopefully, open some parents' eyes. The next time you drop your kid off to play a sport, whatever it might be, you might start to think about whether or not your kid is getting the best possible development. This is our story.

IN THE BEGINNING

Canaan is absolutely crazy football and will play it at every chance he can get, in the house and on the street. I knew he needed to join a football team, but it was important to me his football experience remained fun. I felt it was too soon for him to join a competitive team, but I knew he needed football. I bought Canaan a pair of football boots and I was glad he was getting used to playing in boots on grass. This was important to his development, but I didn't know at the time. Canaan talks about how different it is to play on grass as opposed to playing on AstroTurf. You get different qualities to your development. My partner told me about a group of dads who got together with their kids over at Highbury Park and casually played football.

The dads we met up with were some of the most wonderful people I have ever met. They explained the teams were mixed with kids and dads and the dads were allowed only two touches, then must pass the ball and were not allowed to score goals. I ended up playing too. What a surprise, Canaan loved it! It became a ritual for us every Saturday. Canaan had natural talent, excellent touch, close control, and beautiful dribbling. I would always tell him the top players keep the ball close and under control, and he listened.

'Dribble with your head up and don't be scared to try with your left foot.'

He is right footed. He doesn't have blistering pace, but he makes up for it with his mind. His game intelligence has always been of a high level, and his composure in front of the goal is one of his strengths. He was the only six-year-old who was dribbling around the goalie when scoring a goal. What I didn't know is football scouts in England want you to have blistering pace and power. There seems to be a notion that without these attributes you can't have a career in football. Without pace and power, getting noticed by football scouts in England is almost impossible.

We went to the park consistently for two years. Canaan loved it and got more confident at trying new skills and looked forward to going every Saturday. He was having fun but developing at the same time. When he reached eight years old, I felt it was time for him to join a junior club. I wanted him to get some competitive football and to be part of a team, but that was a new problem.

- How do you find a good junior club?

- How do you find a good junior club with good coaches?

- What makes a good coach?

Trial and error is the only way to know if you are with a good junior club with decent coaches. What makes a good coach? There isn't only one answer to that question. Only experience can determine that. It is crucial a kid's development has structure and you can see and check their progress. Many parents seem to think it doesn't matter and their kid is having fun or it's only casual, but as they get older and start to have a love for the sport and want to take it seriously, their development won't be at the level it should be for their age.

Canaan was out a lot more playing football and often played with the local kids. It turns out one of them liked Canaan and thought he was a good player and even told his mum. His mum approached me and told me about a team called Chapel Boys that her son was playing for at the time. I was then introduced to the coach and was told about the fees and when training was. It was Canaan's first team and he was excited to be part of it and have a kit. This was something he loved, and it didn't change as he got older. He could not contain his excitement for his upcoming first match.

The training consisted of dribbling in and out of the cones, a little jog, and a match. I didn't think the training was bad, but I came to realise it wasn't going to turn Canaan into a technical player and make him comfortable on the ball. I liked the coach as he dealt with the under eights fantastically. His management skills were excellent, but I wasn't seeing enough progress in Canaan's development. I knew we wouldn't be here for the long-term, which was an important decision to make. I would keep looking to find a coach and a team that fitted my philosophy, but, in the meantime, Canaan had his first match.

MATCH DAY

This was going to be Canaan's first experience in competitive football and playing on AstroTurf, but I felt he was more than ready. He had been playing with adults for the last two years and was totally confident and calm. When you have a kid in any sport, you're not just the parent, you are an advisor, physio, coach, driver, and supporter. You want to see them do well, but support is important. There is nothing I love seeing more than Canaan scoring a goal and turning to look at me. It's an amazing feeling.

Market Road is a massive area with eight Astro pitches. We made our way to the pitches, and Canaan found his team and they began warming up. The referee, who was puffing on a cigarette, finished up, called both teams over, and blew his whistle to start the match. I noticed Canaan struggling to keep up with the pace of the game. All this time he had been playing on grass where the ball doesn't roll as quick and the intensity is not as high. I wanted to talk to him but there was no chance to. Then, one of the players was fouled and injured, which gave me the chance to talk to Canaan. I told him he needed to do everything quicker, using one touch or two touches, keep moving and making runs.

'The game will slow down and then you can start doing your dribbling and taking on defenders.'

He smiled at me.

'Thanks, Dad,' and he ran back out onto the pitch.

Maybe if I weren't there he might have got frustrated and ended up having a bad game, but instead he scored two goals and had an excellent debut.

Canaan had now been playing competitive football for a full season. He was going into his second season as an under nine. I wasn't happy with his technical progress. He was doing well in the matches and the coach was happy with him, but I didn't feel he was moving forward technically. This bothered me, but I thought to myself, *Don't worry, something will come.* Into the new season, Canaan's team was scoring lots of goals, beating all comers, and on top of the league. They were unstoppable, until we came up against a team called FDS. When I first saw this team play, I became an instant fan. They were amazing. All the players were comfortable and had a high level of technical ability. Canaan's team could not cope with the skills and dribbling. They passed the ball around like they were adults. They passed the ball from out the back and worked their way up the pitch. No booting high balls. I knew what team Canaan would be playing for next. I later found out FDS was part of a franchise called Brazilian Soccer School. I decided to check them out. They trained four times a week, but the sessions were pay per session. They were encouraged to do as many sessions as they could. Some kids did four sessions a week, others did two sessions a week plus homework. Different skills and ball work were given to the kids to practice in their own time. They had different age groups from under fives to under fifteens in the training sessions. Each age was split into groups and everybody was given their own ball, but not a normal football. They were size 2 balls and were weighty; they didn't bounce high.

The sessions had structure, and the teens and kids enjoyed themselves. There was a lot of banter among the teens to see who had the most skills. It was amazing seeing under sevens and under eights performing skills and looking comfortable on the ball. It made me think Canaan should be on this level. We did practice skills and some drills we got off the internet, but he was behind the level these kids were at. I wanted him to start working with the Brazilian Soccer School as soon as possible, but I didn't want to pull him out of his team mid-season.

The league was a two-horse race between ourselves, Chapel Boys, and the quality side FDS. Canaan was getting stronger with each game and putting in some excellent performances. He is his own biggest critic and sets high standards for himself. When he doesn't have a good game, it ruins his day. Canaan was doing his thing beating defenders effortlessly. He has such quick feet and gets so much joy out of creating a goal.

Chapel Boys was on an unbeaten run and so was FDS. It was all leading up to the big game between ourselves and FDS-the season-defining match; whoever won this game would be crowned as champions. Nervous energy filled the air. I could feel it from the parents and players. It was hard to believe this was an under nines match. I wanted Canaan to do well but I was also looking forward to watching FDS. A mistake by one of the FDS defenders allowed Chapel Boys' striker in, and he slotted the ball into the goal. There was a roar from the parents clapping and celebrating 1-0 to Chapel Boys. Could we beat FDS?

FDS got the match going again after taking kickoff, and it seemed the goal woke them up because they started to play quicker and show more skills. One of the FDS players who was highly developed had some lethal dribbling and change of direction. He caused Chapel Boys all sorts of problems. He kept winning free kicks because he was getting fouled often and, eventually, they scored a goal from one of the free kicks. It was 1-1 all to play for. Watching FDS play was beautiful and so was seeing all those under nines keeping the ball under control, like the ball was stuck to their feet. The momentum was with FDS now. Chapel Boys was struggling to keep the ball. They were going for long spells where they were trying to win the ball and when they did, they lost it again and FDS would keep it. Chapel Boys was being outclassed. It didn't seem fair, but this is football, and that's why I wanted to find the best possible training and coaches for Canaan's development. Chapel Boys ended up losing 2-1. Canaan was disappointed. He wanted to win.

I asked Canaan if he wanted to join FDS and he said yes. He's always up for a new challenge and doesn't mind having to start over and fight for a spot in a new team because he believes he's good enough.

The next day, I wanted to track down the number for Brazilian Soccer School off the internet. I got the number, gave it a call, and got through to the coach of FDS team. I started to explain who I was and that my son played for Chapel Boys. He wanted to know what number shirt Canaan was playing in. I told him number six.

I got the details and looked forward to taking Canaan to his first training session with Brazilian Soccer School. We got there nice and early. I spoke to the coach and explained who I was, and he told Canaan to grab a ball and warm up.

As I mentioned earlier, they don't use normal footballs; they use size 2 footballs and they don't bounce. They use these footballs because they develop your touch and control, and because they are weighty, you keep the football closer to your feet. This also improves dribbling, change of direction, and your overall skills. If you can do skills with a size 2 football it becomes ten times easier to do it with a normal size football.

The session started with them warming up, doing a little jog and some stretching. This was different from our previous club, where the kids went straight into training. It's a good sign when the coach of the club you are at warms up the kids correctly. If your kid is at a junior club and not being warmed up properly, that's a major red flag. After that they were put into groups and everybody had their own ball. This was individual repetitive training. There were three different coaches for each group and different training for different ages. The young ones were shown a skill and then told to practise it while dribbling, and different skills were called out when they had to change. The older groups were put into teams and told to pass the ball to each other and keep it from the other team. There were no goals and the pitch area wasn't very big. This helped develop close control in tight areas with a player marking you. It makes you more comfortable to receive the ball even if a player is marking you, and you are also encouraged to do your skills and not lose it. I thought these training sessions were fantastic, and I was amazed to see how much Canaan improved.

I also found out FDS, the name of the football team, stands for 'Futebol de Salao. Futebol de Salao is a five-a-side version of football of South American origin played with a smaller (size 2), heavier (465g) ball which has virtually no bounce (10%). The game became popular in Brazil, where players such as Pele, Rivelino, Zico, right through to Juninho, Ronaldo, and Rivaldo were brought up first playing Futebol de Salao before moving on to conventional football'.

UNIVERSITY of NORTHUMBRIA

'The university carried out a study comparing training sessions at Brazilian Soccer Schools and those at a professional Football Club's Academy. Whilst at training sessions, the percentage of time the players were engaged "on task" was:

Pro Club-16%

Brazilian Soccer Schools-53%

(The average for elite sports coaching world-wide is around 20-30%) at the time.

Of this "on-task" time, the following statistics were derived from the time spent undertaking "motor appropriate activities"-namely activities which will improve the players at their appropriate level:

Pro Club-33%

Brazilian Soccer School-92%'

www.icfds.com

The Brazilian Soccer School did four training sessions a week at two hours a session. The days you attended were optional. Canaan liked going on the weekends, so he was doing four hours a week. He would also do two hours after school on his own, working on his technique and skills. Sometimes I would get involved and go to the park with him and work on other areas of his game, but he loves taking on players. He knew the difference in kicking the ball ahead of you and chasing it down as opposed to keeping the ball close to your feet and dribbling past players. We don't like kick and chase.

It was beautiful to see Canaan developing. He was playing with confidence at this point. Once the season was over, we went to Highbury Park and met back up with the lads and dads. Canaan was a different player now to when we started lads and dads. He had improved technically, and the dads noticed too. He got compliments all game. He was trying all the skills he had learnt from Brazilian Soccer School and his dribbling was slicker and smoother. The skills would come out, and he was not thinking about doing them; they would come out naturally. We didn't come to lads and dads all the time because it meant Canaan missing training on the Saturday, but he would come sometimes because he knew he had training on the Sunday. I remember the first thing he said to me after his first Brazilian training session.

'How was that, son?'

'That was wicked,' he said

with a big smile on his face.

At Brazilian Soccer School, getting into the football team was different to when we went to Chapel Boys. At Chapel Boys, you pay your fees and come to training, and you're on the team; but, at Brazilian Soccer School, you have to work your way into the team. They had a team of quality players. Canaan knew it would be difficult, but he believed he was good enough to get into the team. They had two teams, FDS A and FDS B. One played in the A league and the other in the B league. Canaan made it onto the B team. It was a step down considering he had been playing in the A league, but he knew he was too good for the B league and it would only be a matter of time before he made it into the A team.

Brazilian Soccer School has a lot of interest, and only some of the kids make it onto the team. Many of the kids came to Brazilian Soccer School to train and play matches with a different team; Canaan was happy to have made it onto the team. Canaan wanted to be on the FDS A team and he was up for the challenge. The coach had told us he would be watching the B league and any players he felt made the grade would be promoted to the A team. It was all Canaan needed to hear. He seems to perform at his best when the pressure is on. He is quite a laid-back character, but he needs to be pushed out of his comfort zone; then he delivers.

A NEW SEASON

After the fees were paid, Canaan had his new kit and new Astro boots and was ready to go. He couldn't wait to try out new skills and to take players on. He knew the quality of players in the B league wasn't going to be as high as the A league. He was still keeping up with his after-school training. Canaan loves football and there were times I had to put my foot down because I felt he was overdoing it. Including his school and training, sometimes he could be doing football six times a week. I had to tell him to rest, which would make him upset, but he understood. He knew I only wanted the best for him and I needed to protect him from himself or he would keep playing if it was left up to him.

Here we were on match day again, but for a new team. Canaan was ready two hours before we had to leave, in his kit waiting to head off. When it was time to leave, I grabbed my coat and Canaan was outside practising with his skill ball.

'Son, it's time to go; put the ball in the house.'

He flicked the ball in the air and curled it into the house with the outside of his foot, and we left. We got to Market Road and I parked the car. Canaan jumped out and ran towards the entrance, shouting.

'Dad, I'm going to find my team.'

As I made my way to the entrance, I saw parents from Chapel Boys. It felt weird not going over to stand with them, but I was with a new team now. It was almost time for kickoff, and we waited for the referee. He was late, but he turned up, looked over to the coaches, then looked at his watch and blew for kickoff. Before I could even get settled, Canaan had picked up a loose ball and drove straight at the defender. The defender dived in with a tackle. Big mistake-he committed himself against my son. Canaan shifted the ball to his left foot, then back to his right foot-this was known as the Zico side sprint-and he was through on goal. When I see Canaan get a one-on-one with the goalkeeper, I always think it's a goal. The goalkeeper tried to make himself big. Canaan took his time and passed the ball into the bottom corner.

'Yes, what a goal!'

There was a lot of clapping and cheering from the other parents and Canaan was beaming. I thought to myself, *If he carries on like this, it shouldn't be long before he gets promoted to the A team.*

Canaan was a constant threat through the whole game. He managed to grab another goal and get an assist. It was a good game all round. We realised the level was not high down in the B league and it was easy for Canaan. He was able to run through the team when he wanted to. He was totally enjoying himself. I knew I didn't want him to stay down in this league for too long. I wanted him back in the A league. The quality of defenders and teams down in the B league was terrible. The level difference between the two leagues was massive. After Canaan had been running rampant in the B league for two months, the coach promoted him to the A team. Another one of the players was to be promoted too. Finally, back in the A league, Canaan was ecstatic.

The coach wanted Canaan to play as a striker. He had been playing striker or winger, but we took it as high praise as FDS was the highest scoring team in the league. They had plenty of options for a striker. He was still trying to find his best position.

It had taken Canaan two months to get into the FDS A team. All good, right? Wrong. Here's where we started to have problems. It had been a smooth ride since he started playing football. He walked straight into the Chapel Boys' team and established himself quickly, moved to FDS B and did the same, but this time he was going into a team of champions, which was filled with many talented players, and they had a big squad. On match day you could have nearly two teams and coaches generally stick with the players performing. Should a coach sub a player performing because he wants to give another player some game time? Coaches are put under serious pressure by parents when their kid is on the sideline and not getting game time, but both the parent and the coach have rights. The coach should be allowed to pick his team and play the players he wants or who have earned their spot on the team, but parents who have paid their club fees, wherever the match may be held, will want to see their kid playing football and not stuck on the sidelines getting frustrated.

Canaan knew it wouldn't be as easy to establish himself on the team, but he was up for the challenge. He has such a belief in himself and looked forward to his first match with the main team. At this point, I felt he was progressing all the time and enjoying his football. Everything was about him, not me. Match day came again, his debut for his new team, and he wanted to start with a bang. I was the driver and advisor. On the way to Market Road, we discussed his game. I told him to pick his moments when he took on defenders.

We got to Market Road and after about ten minutes, Canaan came onto the pitch with his team. There were enough players to make two teams.

He was started on the bench when the match began, a new experience for him and one he is not used to, but he always knew he would have to earn his way into the team. It didn't take long for FDS to get into their flow. It was amazing watching these under tens knock the ball around and the other team chasing them. They couldn't get the ball. FDS was two goals up quickly. Half time came and went, and Canaan still hadn't come on. Then, with about five minutes left of the match, Canaan finally came on and he did not look happy. He barely got a touch of the ball before the whistle was blown and the match was over. Some of the players never even got to play. After the match, we talked, and I told him to stay positive.

'You're good enough to force your way on the team.'

But it never changed. Canaan was not able to get any consistency going, and it affected his confidence. He needs to feel wanted and trusted in his ability. An arm around the shoulder will go much further than a bollocking. This is where man management skills are crucial. A coach can get his point across without having to shout at the kids.

Canaan was going into under elevens for the next season, and we had a decision to make about what team he stayed on. I didn't want to teach him when the going gets tough you quit; I wanted him to keep developing. After Canaan and I had a good talk, we decided he would join another team but continue his training with Brazilian Soccer School.

His school was picking players for the school team, and I had a coach from Pro Touch Academy, who had been after Canaan from when he was at Chapel Boys. His name was Sam. Canaan had been playing football in the park while the older age group of Pro Touch Academy had been training. They saw Canaan, called him over, and told him to join in and were impressed with him holding his own against the older boys. They took my number and gave it to Sam. Sam rang me a couple days later and wanted me to come down and have a session with him to see Canaan, but I explained he had a team and was happy. We always kept in contact and he would phone me to see how Canaan was.

After a few months of talking with Sam, I told him Canaan was looking for a new team and he gave me the details for when training was. Canaan was feeling a bit down about having to leave FDS because he had worked hard to get into the team. He did not want another season of being a fringe player, which he felt was due to the size of the squad and not his performance. I felt his performances had been good with the limited time he was striving to be the best. I am proud of the way Canaan conducts himself when it comes to his football. As he got older, I didn't have to motivate him too much. He is disciplined about the type of food he eats. He goes jogging with his mum and attends fitness classes, and these are all his own decisions. I advise him what I think is right and wrong, but I let him make up his own mind and learn from his own mistakes. I always tell him becoming a footballer is not just about playing football. It's the whole lifestyle of constantly working on yourself to get better. I told Canaan that Sam was looking forward to seeing him and had heard nothing but good things. After he looked down, a nice smile appeared on his face and I smiled back.

TRAINING FOR A NEW TEAM

Training was in Kings Cross and it was pouring down with rain. The amount of early mornings I have spent standing in the rain or freezing my arse off is too many times to count, but I need to be there to support him, and I love doing it. It was a little pitch inside a cage. We saw some other children and a young guy with them. The guy turned to us and, coming over, introduced himself as Sam. He was no older than nineteen or twenty. Canaan went off and got a ball while Sam told me about his ideas and his philosophy. He was enthusiastic about coaching. You could feel he loved it.

Sam started the sessions off with the players doing a warm-up and stretching, which was a sign of a good coach. It should be common sense a coach should warm up the players, but sadly it's not. After Sam had warmed up the players, he went straight into ball work, splitting them into little groups with one player in the middle and the other players passing the ball around, keeping it away from the player in the middle. If the player in the middle managed to win the ball, the person who lost the ball went into the middle. I had seen this drill before at Brazilian Soccer School.

Sam believed you need to develop the players to be technically comfortable on the ball before you can make the players play a passing style of football. His training sessions were ball work, ball work, and more ball work, and Canaan loved it. These training sessions were perfect for him. He was still doing his sessions with Brazilian Soccer School, but this was a bonus and Canaan took to the training like a duck to water. This was Sam's first time seeing Canaan in the flesh, and he thought he should be in an academy. He was the first person to say it to me, but he was not the last. Canaan has never been bothered about getting into an academy. He would love to do it to gain the experience, but if a coach attempted to change the player he is, he would leave immediately.

Sam was finishing up his training session. After he had ended the session, he came over to me to make sure Canaan was happy and wanted to come back. His team was the Pro Touch Community team, and there were a lot of players new to football or looking to give football a try. He wanted Canaan to play for him for a little while and then move into the Pro Touch Academy team. Players are put into the academy team from the community team if they are good enough. Canaan and I were fine with this. He knew the quality was not high after coming from a team like FDS, but he didn't care. He wanted to play football, and Sam told us we would be playing in the Regents Park League. This meant being back on grass, and Canaan absolutely loves grass. He is at his most comfortable playing football on grass. For the last three years, he had been playing football on AstroTurf, so he was excited about playing on grass again.

Canaan made captain on his school team and he was beaming. This was a new responsibility for him and good for his development. He would get a chance to develop his leadership skills. Some players are born with natural leadership skills, some are not. Canaan is not a natural leader on the field, but he doesn't mind taking on more responsibility. He is always the first to step up for a penalty or free kick. The school football team was coached by Mr Lannigan.

Mr Lannigan was a fantastic guy from Australia and had been teaching at Canaan's school for a few years. We hit it off straight away. I explained to him about what the district coach had told me. He told me they had only come one time for players and had stopped coming. I told him to expect an invite for trials with the district team and, from that moment, I became a part of the school football team. I went to all the games to help with all the players. Canaan was having an excellent season with his school team. He took to the role of being captain and loved it. At the same time, with his club team, Pro Touch Academy, he played at a high level and had made captain in his second game. He was scored for his club and school, but the players in his school team were much better than the players at his club team. He racked up lots of assists for his school team and played with a high level of confidence. One of Canaan's strengths is his dribbling. When he plays at the top of his game, he can glide past players. He is also strong and difficult to knock off the ball.

As parents, we can sometimes delude ourselves into thinking our kids are better than they are. I believe Canaan is an excellent player, full of potential, but we have worked on his game and don't stop working at it. He knows he is not the fastest player or the most dynamic and, in England, pace and power seem to be the only attributes wanted, but Canaan is not bothered. He knows what he is up against and he knows he will offer football teams a different quality. He's willing to play football abroad if it comes to it. He will go to a country where they are looking more for the type of player he is. He wants to be the type of player that is clever, tricky, and inventive. The type of player England doesn't produce enough of. The type of player who can do something amazing and win football matches on his own.

Barcelona FC had won the Champions League final, and I was amazed at how, during the match, Barcelona FC kicked the ball long aimlessly about three or four times. All the other times the ball went long it was to a player. The ball never went back to the goalkeeper, and if it did, it was so Barcelona FC could keep possession of the ball. Canaan wants to be able to play for Barcelona FC one day, but wanting to play for a team like Barcelona FC and having power and pace is not going to be enough. There are many more attributes you need to have if you want to play for Barcelona FC.

DISTRICT TRIALS

The district trials were being held at Market Road by two coaches: Mike and Warren. They explained it was to be a six-week process and matches were to be played simultaneously. They would be going around and watching the players, plus also mixing up the matches. They said they would be cutting players and calling back players at the end of each day. Canaan wanted to get in and he was in good form for his club and school. He wasn't worried one bit.

Four matches were being played at the same time, and there were some good players. They had come from schools all over Islington, and most of the players were in a club or playing for their school football team. There were a lot of talented players all desperate to make the district team. The trials got started and Canaan was performing at a high level, but he was forcing the skills a bit. I had a quick word in his ear to remind him about his decision-making.

'Use your skills at the right time; stop forcing it.'

He relaxed, and his decision-making got better. When I am not happy with something in his game, I have a quiet word with him. Shouting and screaming doesn't help. Canaan and I have had arguments after some matches where I have thought he played shit, but it is done in the car drive home or at home, not when he is playing in the match.

The trials for the day were coming to an end. Mike called the players over and separated them into groups. He told all the players he had seen some good players and wanted everyone to come back. Nobody was cut the first week.

A parent told me trials were happening at another location as well because they had many players. I am not sure if this was true. Trials were every week and Canaan was asked to come back. The number of players was getting smaller as they were getting cut. Eventually, we got down to the last week of trials. The session for the trial matches started, and all the players left played at a high level. I had felt Canaan should go through on all the weeks before, but on this day, I was a bit unsure. Canaan was still playing well, but the quality of the defenders he played against was high level, and he had to do everything even quicker. By now, the players knew him and knew he had quick feet and was clever, so he was not given any space. Players got tight to him and doubled up on him. This is where all the mentoring and teaching comes in. When players were getting tight, he upped his movement and limited his touches of the ball to find space to dribble. When players were doubling up, he looked for the pass. He adapted to what was unfolding on the pitch. I was happy he was remembering the things we talked about and implementing them on the pitch. We are always going over his game, and we watch *Match of the Day* together and see what we can learn and add to his game. He takes it seriously, I take it seriously. He wants to have a career in football, whether at the top level of football or not. The trials came to an end. Mike and Warren put the players into groups, and Warren took the group Canaan was in. Mike had the other groups. The players were told to sit down, and Mike and Warren spoke to their groups.

At this point, I was nervous. I thought Canaan had played well, but it was his hardest trial day. I was unsure if he had made the squad or not. After Warren and Mike had spoken to the groups for about fifteen minutes, there was a loud cheer from my son's group. He had made the squad and he was ecstatic. Two other boys from Canaan's school had made the squad too. Drayton Park School had three players in the district team for the first time. Canaan getting into the squad made me happy, but two other boys from Canaan's school getting in too was excellent. They were two boys we knew well. Mike called the parents over and explained matches would be coming thick and fast. Training would be on a Thursday and the team would be picked based on training. Mike was efficient and organised. He did not mess about.

Mike is short for Michael. He is an FA Level 3 Coach (UEFA 'B' Licence). He has over twenty-five years of coaching experience and works for Islington Football Development Partnership, mainly focusing on football schemes and facility renewal projects. He is also youth sports development manager for Islington Council. He has worked as a scout for various professional clubs for the past seventeen years.

Warren is also an FA Level 3 Coach (UEFA 'B' Licence.) He was working full-time as a football development officer for the Islington Football Development Partnership. He has been coaching for seven years and has also played at semi-professional level.

Canaan being selected for the district team only made his confidence grow. It was nice to get some recognition from coaches with some credentials. It helped reinforce what we were doing was right. Mike told me Canaan was tricky and clever and would offer something different to the team. He believed he would be important to unlocking tight defences. This is what Canaan wants-to develop into a creative player, otherwise known as a number ten or an attacking midfielder. At the time, we hadn't started honing his game to play any specific role. He still played different positions, mainly striker and winger, but he always came alive when he could play off a striker. Canaan likes players around him who will make runs and have lots of movement.

I was looking forward to seeing what training for the district team would be like. I wondered what Mike and Warren's philosophy was. Ever since Canaan and I came across Brazilian Soccer School, we tried to stick with coaches who had a similar philosophy, who encourage players to express themselves and don't give a bollocking when it doesn't go well. Some junior clubs Canaan has tried out for didn't have our philosophy. I want more parents to think like this and not accept mediocrity. It can only be good for grassroots football and sport. Canaan was playing a lot of football, and you always wonder as a parent whether it is too much. We had to explain to his junior club coach, Sam, Canaan had made the district team and it was going to clash with his matches. Sam was not happy to lose his captain, but he understood. He was happy for Canaan and told us he deserved it.

Some coaches have an ego and don't want to be told anything, or they are a part-time coach. They only care about winning and don't care about how the players are developing. That's one of the biggest problems I see at grassroots football: coaches with no philosophy or style of play. They get a team full of big, tall kids and tell them to kick the ball long, and because these coaches get results, they have no reason to change what they're doing. I don't know how the kids are supposed to develop if the football is always in the air. Canaan does not do well with this type of football. I have coached him to keep the ball on the ground, to pick out players, and to move after passing the ball. He likes football played on the ground and that has helped him become the player he is. If a coach wants to have a long ball style, it is his choice. Long ball can be effective. Coaches have made a career playing this style of football. Junior clubs should make it clear to parents what their style and philosophy are.

Coaches who want to play the passing game and keep the ball on the ground want kids who are technically comfortable on the ball and confident to receive and pass the ball. The development of the kids will go in that direction. I personally believe the passing game is the best form of development for the kids. When junior clubs employ this philosophy, the kids seem to develop better and so does the team. We can go into all the attributes being developed-passing, touch, control, decision-making, and I could go on-but I struggle to see the developing side of long ball for the kids. The ball is in the air more, which means fewer touches. When the ball is kicked long from the defence, it means the midfield is missed out and the ball goes long to the strikers. You need kids big, strong, and good at heading the ball.

PLAYING FOR THE DISTRICT TEAM

Mike and Warren made it clear they would not be doing fitness training. They knew all the players were in junior clubs and felt the fitness training got from their clubs was enough. They wanted to focus on passing drills, ball work, and tactics. They believed in the passing philosophy and wanted the ball to be kept on the ground. Once you know a coach's philosophy, it can give you peace of mind knowing how your kid will be developed with them. Some coaches will tell you they believe in the pass and move philosophy, but then they do something totally different and are not congruent with their words. Once training had finished, Mike went around handing out pieces of paper with all the match details on it. The players who got one had been selected for the squad, for the weekend game. Canaan had got one and he was happy. The first game would be against Thurrock; this meant we would have to be travelling to Essex. This was the furthest I would have travelled with Canaan for football, but we were looking forward to it.

On the day of the match, Mike took the players off to get changed and then led them out onto the pitch to warm up. The pitch was beautiful, and you could see it had been taken care of. It made the whole occasion feel like this Canaan was playing at a higher level. I was getting more caught up in the occasion than my son. Canaan remained calm and level-headed. He took it as another game of football. The pitch was massive, and the goals were full-size. It was the first time Canaan had played with full-size goals and in an eleven-a-side team with offside. He started on grass and played on grass with his junior club, but the goals were smaller, and they played teams of eight-a-side. This was a fantastic experience and brilliant for his development. Canaan was looking forward to testing himself against higher-level defenders. After about fifteen minutes more of Mike warming up the players, the referee came onto the pitch and called the captains of both teams over and flipped a coin. Thurrock won the coin toss. They decided they would play from left to right. The players got into positions. Canaan was not starting, but he was too far away to talk to. He was over on the other side with Warren and the other substitutes. Mike had to run the line and Warren was doing the coaching. The referee looked over at the linesmen and then blew his whistle for kickoff.

Islington started off exceptionally, played some excellent football through all thirds of the pitch, and nearly took the lead. A corner was taken quickly, and from the resulting cross, the ball was fired over.

Shortly after, Islington took the lead. The ball was fired across the ground, in the box, and then knocked into the goal, with a left foot finish by the striker. There were cheers and clapping from the parents. Canaan was desperate to get on. Islington continued to dominate. Warren was keeping the substitutes warmed up on the sidelines. He called Canaan and notified the referee Warren was making a substitution.

Straight away, Canaan came onto the pitch and, within two minutes, he'd picked up the ball and dribbled straight at the defender. He beat him, and another defender dived in with a sliding tackle. Canaan skipped over the tackle. At this point, he should have maybe passed, but there was one more defender and if he had got past him, he would have been through on goal; but he got tackled and the ball went out for a throw-in. The better option was for him to pass, but we want kids to be inventive and express themselves and not be afraid to take on two or three defenders. I like Canaan taking on defenders, but I always tell him to pick his moments and it is still about good decision-making. If you try to do something one or two times and it doesn't work out, try different things. Make sure you react in the right way when something you try does not come off.

Once half time was over, the referee called the players over to kickoff the second half. All the players got into their positions, and the referee blew his whistle to get the second half underway. It seems like the coach of Thurrock had got his players going because they came out with a different purpose and immediately put Islington on the back foot. Thurrock scored two early goals. They were starting to dominate, and Islington couldn't get going. Islington was on the back foot for most of the second half, every now and then having some good counter-attacks, but in the last eight minutes of the game, Thurrock scored three more goals and the final score ended up being 5-1, which I felt was unfair. Islington did not deserve to lose with that score line. Mike got the players together and made them do a warm-down. He told them there were plenty of positives to take from the game, plus a couple of good lessons in making sure we keep our heads in the game and make our dominance count with goals.

It was Canaan's first taste of district football, and I was the proudest father. Canaan was cool, calm, and collected. For him, it was another football match. I have seen Canaan score some amazing goals, and I have gone ballistic but he is cool about it, like it's another goal and another day. It doesn't go to his head. We have come a long way from playing lads and dads over at Highbury Park. Canaan was representing his borough.

There was a district game every week. The next game would be against Westminster. Westminster was coached by Sam Essien. Mike explained Sam should be congratulated on his sterling work in reviving Westminster's primary district team, which had not run for several years. District football relies mainly on volunteers. I believe district football is another important avenue to bring through talented footballers. District football has a long tradition of providing opportunities for boys and girls to play competitive football, and the primary district team is the first opportunity for them to play representative football. With all the government cuts at the time, which included school sports partnerships, it is even more important the personnel and organisations supporting this level of football, which are mainly voluntary, continue to exist to support school football.

The game was to be played at St Aloysius Playing Field. This was one of our home venues. I knew the boys were disappointed with how they lost last week against Thurrock. They felt they should have got something out of the game. They were pumped for this game.

After Warren had got the players warmed up, he told the players who was starting, and Canaan was one of them. The referee blew his whistle and got the match underway. Islington was straight on top and came close with a shot which went past the post of the opposing goal. Our goalie made a fantastic save. It was a scorpion kick. The ball had gone over his head and he saved it with the back of his heels and flicked away the ball from danger. Islington was totally on top, but the goal would not come, and the referee blew the whistle for half time. I couldn't hear the team talk, but I assume the players were told to keep doing what they were doing, and the goal would come. I was hoping they didn't get disheartened, because they were playing well. Half time was over and the referee blew for the second half. Islington kept the pressure up and, five minutes into the second half, Canaan latched onto a pass outside the box, did a quick turn, created the space, and shot. This caught the goalkeeper off guard and the ball was in the back of the net. There was a loud cheer from the parents. I was over the moon. Canaan had scored his first district goal and he was celebrating with his teammates. He was playing as a second striker and loved the role. I was happy with his development. We were now seeing the benefits of all the hard work he had put into improving his technical ability. He had no problem controlling the ball and stopping it dead in its tracks. He could take the ball out of the air and have it under control instantly. He still had areas of his game which he needed to work on, like his heading. I also felt he needed to be braver when going into challenges, but as he got older, those attributes got better. I am his dad, I can be a bit biased, but I thought he was turning into an excellent player.

The referee blew his whistle for Westminster to take centre and get the match underway again. Islington was not giving them any time on the ball. Five minutes later, Islington scored again. A nice ball for the midfielder and he was through on goal and buried the ball right into the bottom corner. Another cheer from the parents and clapping. At this point, Islington was cruising. They were not done. They kept up the pressure and, two minutes later, the other striker got another goal with an excellent finish. Islington was rampant. We thought they had scored again with a glancing header, but the ball ran through a hole in the net and the referee did not give it. Islington was not stopping this pressure, and we had a number of shots going wide. Westminster had a couple of counter attacks, and our defender had to clear the ball off the line to keep Islington's clean sheet. The referee finally blew his whistle for full time. The game finished 3-0. I thought Islington was excellent; Mike felt the team started okay and were a bit out of shape, but they stepped up a gear in the second half. He also mentioned the first half against Thurrock last week was excellent, but the match today was a more consistent performance throughout.

At an academy, you could be doing well and then find yourself released because they think you are too small or not quick enough. It should be on talent and performance. If you're performing, who cares you're not big like a giant or fast like an Olympic runner? It's one of the reasons Canaan is going to keep his options open and be prepared to move abroad, where it's not all about the biggest and fastest. I would like to see more English players go abroad. If being a big and fast player was the only way to become a footballer, then I wouldn't have any argument. Some of the highest quality players in the Premier League are not the biggest. They're not always the fastest. Canaan is an Arsenal fan and loves Mesut Özil. Özil is not the fastest or the strongest, but he is a world-class player because his other attributes are amazing, such as his vision, intelligence, touch, technical ability, passing, and ability to read the game. England does not produce enough of these types of players, or maybe scouts aren't looking for these types of players. Canaan believes he is good enough to have a career in football. His ultimate goal would be to get to the top of English football, but he still believes he can have a career in football regardless. When he plays, he creates goals, he scores goals, and that's what your coach wants; it's what your club want. He knows if he keeps performing at the highest level possible, then it will only be a matter of time before someone appreciates him for the player he is.

Canaan's next game was against Brent, and it was such a horrible day. It would not stop raining. The pitch was muddy but still playable. Canaan started this match, but he struggled to get into the game. It was not one of his best games and he was substituted in the second half. He was disappointed with himself and had tears in his eyes. We went for a walk while the match was playing, and I told him not to worry.

The match finished 1-1 and that was a tough, grinding game for Islington. I think Islington was happy to get the draw. Canaan was not selected for the next two fixtures: Tower Hamlet away and a Sainsbury seven-a-side competition. He was disappointed but was looking forward to meeting back up with his junior club. Going down to Regents Park felt strange. To Canaan, it was more football. If it wasn't going to be for his district team, then it would be for his junior club. We met up with his teammates and they were happy to see him. They asked him lots of questions about how the district games were going. Canaan was happy to see his teammates and it was good for him to forget about his disappointment with the district team. He was looking forward to the game. He knew the Regents Park League was nowhere near the same level of district football; it gave him an air of confidence going into the game.

Sam and I spoke, and I also met his new assistant, Chris. These guys were nice and passionate about coaching. Young guys trying to develop their style and the type of football they wanted to play. To develop the training that would get them to their goal. There is a problem I often see with young coaches and coaches in general. Once they have their coaching badges, they are now qualified to develop kids. They don't continue to grow as a coach and develop their style. If what they are doing gets results and wins football matches, why continue to develop and grow? But, as I have mentioned before and will mention again, because a coach is winning football matches does not mean that the kids are developing, and that should be the number one priority.

The match kicked off and Canaan was on fire; his dribbling was decisive and powerful, and the opposing team could not get the ball off him. He was definitely in the mood. Canaan was doing through ball after through ball and constantly splitting up the opposing defence, but many of his teammates were inexperienced. Moves broke down and the team was not getting the rewards. Eventually, Canaan created his own chance and scored a goal. He was doing skills and was a constant menace to the opposite team. As the game wore on, the opposing players started to double up on Canaan and crowded him out anytime he was near the ball. It got more difficult for him to keep on having the same impact. Canaan's team ended up losing 5-2.

After the match finished, the players shook hands and the opposing coach spoke to Sam. Sam came over and told me the coach told him he thought Canaan was a fantastic player and was one of the most technical players he had seen in his whole time being a coach. That put a big smile on my face. It's what I set out to do: to make sure Canaan was technically comfortable on the ball and to give him the best possible chance of becoming a footballer. It's the fundamentals which are important when developing as a football player. These have to be taught to the kids when they are young. As they get older, it becomes a natural part of their game.

Canaan uses his sole, laces, outside of the foot; he is not as comfortable on the left foot as he is on his right foot, but he is constantly working on his left foot. These are some of the fundamentals that should start to be developed when players are young kids. It should be compulsory for coaches working with young kids to develop them to become comfortable using their left foot and right foot and technically comfortable on the ball. In school, there is a curriculum and teachers know their pupils should be at a certain level by a certain time or age, but at grassroots football, there is nothing. It's free for all and coaches can do what they want and are generally more concerned about winning, not the kids' development. I find it disturbing when a kid has been at a junior club for years and they have no touch, no control, can't shoot, can't pass. It's not good enough and it's not being addressed.

Sam told me he wanted to push Canaan through to the academy team. He didn't want to lose him, but he felt he was too good to be playing for the community team. Canaan was fine with it. He likes to play with players who can help him improve. He has always been more comfortable playing with players older than him and can get frustrated when he plays with players not of a certain standard. Either way, he was happy to be playing for his district team and was more than happy to continue playing for Sam if the academy team never came through.

I was happy with Canaan's development and wanted his development to keep going forward in the right way. Technically, he was developing nicely, but I always knew this was just one aspect of his development and I wanted him to develop into a well-rounded player. This is where it got a bit difficult because I knew what I wanted but was not sure how to develop his in-game attributes, his movement and runs. At the time, he had not settled into a position. He was played as a striker the majority of the time. We now know Canaan is not an out-and-out striker. As a matter of fact, he doesn't like the role. He likes to play in a system which is fluid and not structured. In England, a lot of the coaches play a structured system and want players to stay in their position and not move but wait around for the ball. When a kid decides to leave his position, and goes looking for the ball, he gets a bollocking and is substituted. How is this any good for a player's confidence? Canaan does not do well when he is told to stay in his spot and not move. Coaches will tell players to stay in their position and not move, and if a player complains, the coach will tell the kid they are not being disciplined. It takes the fun and joy out of playing football. I would like football to stay fun for Canaan for as long as possible.

Canaan was doing well with his education. He was a good student, which made things easier with his football. He knew, if at any point his education started to slip, it would affect his football. I made it clear his education was number one priority. He also knew how serious we take his education; I am not one of those dads crazy about my son getting top marks in his exams. I want him to do his best at whatever he does. I left school with no qualifications and here I am writing a book. Canaan tells his teachers he wants to be a footballer, and they look at him like he is crazy or it's impossible. Everything he hears is a negative attitude. They want him to say a 'normal job'. It's where I have a different attitude from his teachers. If you work hard and totally believe in yourself, you can accomplish anything. I try to inspire Canaan to achieve what he truly wants out of life, and he wants to become a footballer. It has not changed from him starting out when he was six to now, at fifteen. All that has happened is he has become more dedicated, focused, and confident in his abilities. I will do everything in my power to help him achieve his goal. If he wanted to be a doctor, it would be the same attitude.

Canaan had been training with his district team. The second week of not getting selected for his district team hit him quite hard. He knew it meant going back down to Regents Park to join up with his junior club. I tried to keep his spirits up. It was hard. I could tell he was missing playing district football. Saturday always seems to come around quite quickly, and it was the same routine, water, shin pads, and football boots. It was never a drag for him. We got to Regents Park and I was met by Sam and Chris. They told me the under fourteens academy coach was here to watch the game. I told Canaan about the academy coach being here, and he looked forward to the game even more. The match kicked off and Canaan was in no mood to mess about. They were playing the top team in the league, but it did not matter. They could not take the ball off Canaan. His dribbling was immense. He was gliding past players with ease. He didn't try to run past players; he beat them, he sucked defenders in to make the tackle and skipped past them. Canaan was a constant menace with his quick feet and skills. His team ended up losing. The opposing team had a fantastic player too. The type of player I like: intelligent, with an excellent ability to pop up in the box and score goals. He was not quick, didn't have blistering pace, but his mind was quick, and he was sharp.

After the match ended, the academy coach came and spoke to me. He told me Canaan was a good player and wanted to push him into the academy. He took my number and told me he would call me. As we were heading home, I got talking to another coach. I then realised it was the opposing coach.

I started talking about the player I liked in his team and how I thought he was a top player. The coach started to explain how he was battling with the head coach to keep him on the team, because the head coach thought he was not big enough. He told me they were not looking at the fact that he was an intelligent player and had excellent movement and was one of the highest goal scorers on the team. All they were looking at was the fact that he was not big. I spoke to the coach a little bit more and then wished him well and we left. In England, we have an obsession with players that are full of pace and big and strong. We are obsessed with direct football and crossing in the box, even though we know that this football is not effective on the international stage. We are a prideful country and our culture and pride inhibit us from change. I want England to win the World Cup in my lifetime. I would love to experience that feeling. In England, we produce players that are suited for the Premier League, big, strong, powerful, pacey players, and we end up having the same type playing for the national team.

I want to see England produce all different types of players. I believe there is a big problem with the amount of English talent coming through the academies. When they do come through, they are all the same type of player. I want to see more inventive and clever players coming through, intelligent players and match winners.

Canaan had his mind on the next district match all week. He was nervous because he wanted to be selected for the next match, and he was looking to work his socks off in training. When the training session came to an end, Mike gave out the slips to the players who had been selected, and Canaan got one. He was happy. He couldn't stop smiling.

The next match was going to be against Woolwich at our home ground. Canaan was focused. He went to bed early and was up early. We left the house earlier than I wanted to, but Canaan could not contain himself. Canaan wanted to get to the home ground early to warm up. When we got to the ground, Mike and Warren were not there yet. A few players were having a kick about and Canaan decided to go join them. The home ground was the Douglas Eyre Sports Centre. The pitches had been taken care of beautifully. I have not been to many grounds where there are tractors and grounds men. The Douglas Eyre Sports Centre had a little cafeteria where you could buy some hot snacks and hot drinks. I was sitting in the cafeteria looking around. Trophies and medals were everywhere. As I finished up my tea, I saw Mike come in through the door. He came over to me and greeted me and then headed out to the pitch. I decided to go and find Canaan. He hadn't moved from where I'd left him, and he had been joined by the majority of his teammates. Warren was also there.

It felt like a big turnout. The weather had been terrible, so on other days there had not been as many parents as normal. However, on this particular day, there were a lot of parents. I was constantly saying hello to someone. It was almost kickoff and Mike and Warren had been warming up the players. The referee was ready to kick off the match. Many of the parents had been in the cafeteria and had now come out onto the pitch to watch the match. *This will help give it a nice atmosphere,* I thought. The referee blew his whistle and got the match underway. Not even five minutes on the clock when Canaan closed down a player and won the ball. He then beat another player and delivered a beautiful through ball that split the opposing defence and landed right onto the midfielder's foot, who made an excellent run into the box and buried the ball into the bottom corner of the goal.

There was a loud scream and cheer from the parents. You could see the confidence flow through the Islington boys and Canaan was definitely in the mood. His teammates must have felt it too because the ball kept being passed to him. He beat two players and delivered another beautiful through ball with the outside of his foot. It curled deliciously into the striker's path and he blasted it into the goal. There was more screaming from the parents and lots of clapping and cheering. This pass was almost identical to the first pass but with the outside of the foot. All these years of him working on his ball work and learning to manipulate the ball with different parts of his foot was paying off: using his instep, outside, sole, and lace. If he wanted the ball to behave in a certain way, he knew what part of the foot to use. If he wanted to curl the ball outward, he would use his instep to finish in front of the goal, knowing he would get more accuracy to put the ball into the corners of the goal. If he wanted the ball to curl inward, he would use the outside of his foot, and, if he wanted power, he would use his lace. He would also use his instep to pass the ball, but if he wanted to chip the ball or lob it, he would use his lace. He could also chip the ball with his instep. And with his sole, he would stop the ball and drag the ball. Also, doing all the ball work made him comfortable to try flicks and back heels.

Canaan was an absolute menace to the opposing team. They were struggling to contain him. His skills and quick feet were entertaining the parents on the sidelines. The ball was passed across the field and intercepted by an Islington player, who then passed it to my son. Canaan picked up the ball and drove straight at the opposing defence. He then stopped, had a little look, and chipped the ball over the defender's head and into the oncoming path off the midfielder's run. The midfielder took a shot, but the goalkeeper pulled off a good save and pushed the ball out for a corner. There were oohs and aahs from the parents. Canaan wanted his goal and, in the second half, he eventually got his chance. He picked up the ball near the opposing box, beat a defender, and blasted the ball into the roof of the net. He ran off celebrating with his teammates. I had the biggest smile on my face. I was happy for him. The parents were clapping and cheering too. He got substituted before the end of the match and got a massive round of applause from the parents. Mike came over and shook his hand and told him well done.

From that moment on, Canaan only got stronger for the district team. He was involved in all the rest of the games of the season. Sometimes he started and sometimes he came on as a substitution. He was playing at a high level and I was proud of him. Another game I remember was when Islington was not playing well. They looked disjointed and the passing was not flowing. Canaan came on from the bench and got the team playing football by spreading the ball and keeping the ball moving. From that moment on, Islington was a different team; but it was subtle, the influence Canaan had on the game. Mike noticed it because we spoke about it after the match. Would a scout see that? Are they looking for that? Every time a scout is interested in a player, it is because he's either big or strong or because he has blistering pace. What happened to signing a player because he is talented? Nowadays, you have to tick certain boxes, or they are not interested. We see players getting released from academies all the time and going on to have a career in football. The system is flawed. It's a numbers game; bring in a load of players and then see if any of them are good enough and release the rest. I am not a fan of academies. I prefer players to hone their game by playing competitive football and to develop their unique style. I hear a lot of coaches in the academies don't like players with skills and trickery. Parents I have met at Brazilian Soccer School have pulled their kid from football academies because they see changes happening in their development. Kids are not allowed to express themselves and are being taught to keep it simple.

Canaan finished the season in top form. He received player of the season for his school team and lots of different medals. Islington District team won the Tower Hamlet Cup, and this was their first piece of silverware in six seasons. Islington had an excellent football team with some cracking players. Every player deserved to be on the team. The only sad thing is that most of the players don't play football anymore. They couldn't keep up the motivation to go and play for a junior club again. The level of football was too low, and they needed to play for a higher-level team after district. There was no problem with players coming and training or being motivated for the district team, but they struggled to get the same motivation for a junior club. A lot of the players ended up losing interest and giving football up. I get to see what is going on with grassroots football because I am a part of it. Sometimes, I feel the heads at the top of the game have lost touch with what is going on. Canaan was looking forward to playing for the district team next season, but it wouldn't be Mike and Warren doing it. They only did under elevens; it would be coached by a new coach.

All of Canaan's football was coming to an end. I never did hear back from the Pro Touch Academy coach to put Canaan into the academy. Sam went back to university and his assistant, Chris, took over another team. Canaan would be looking for a new junior club for the new season. Mr Lannigan, who was the coach of Canaan's school football team, moved back to Australia. Canaan was also starting his new secondary school; he was excited and also looking forward to checking out the school football team. The search was on for a new junior club, and it was a difficult job. As you know by now, I don't want to put Canaan just anywhere. I want a club that will help me to continue his development. Many of the club coaches I spoke to would talk about how much they won but not about the development side. When I talk to a coach, I can usually tell by their language what is important to them.

When they start going on about how many trophies they have won and nothing about the style of play or development, I know it's time to move on. Also, you will have coaches who will tell you what you want to hear. Coaches aren't stupid, and they know most people love football played the beautiful way and will tell parents what they want to hear. What I usually do is find out where they are training and playing matches and go and check them out. A number of times a coach has told me they play pass and move and it's all about the kid's development, but when I go and watch a match or check out their training session, I am totally disappointed. I don't know how many parents are doing their own due diligence.

Canaan was known locally because he had played for FDS and also represented Islington; I was not short of offers from junior clubs. I was not happy with any of them. They knew Canaan was a good player and were more interested in what he could do for them than in how they could help him. Canaan wanted to get into his new team as soon as possible. He wanted to make sure he got all the pre-season training, and he was working with his mum on his fitness. He was getting a little bit concerned we had not found a team yet. I told him not to worry because the right team would come up. Canaan ended up speaking to one of his friends from his school and district team. He was a cracking player and was released by Watford FC for being too small. He lived not too far from Canaan and would sometimes play out with him. When Canaan told him he was looking for a team, he got excited and told his mum straight away. His mum was excited too and told me the team was called Isledon Wolves. She told me she would let the club owner know of our interest. She also told me about the coach, whose name was Adrian, and she thought he was a good coach. Isledon Wolves were playing at Market Road, and I was definitely going to go check them out.

Canaan wanted to check out the team too, so he and I headed up to Market Road. When we got there, it seemed like a lot was going on. I saw Canaan's friend's mum again. She introduced me to the club owner. He was a cool guy. He told me where training was and the times, and we walked over to where Isledon Wolves were playing. I only watched Isledon Wolves for ten minutes, and I knew this was the team I wanted Canaan to play for next. The goalkeeper never kicked the ball upfield. When the goalkeeper had the ball, his right and left defenders would split, and the goalkeeper had a choice of which defender to throw it to. The right or left player of midfield would come across to support the defender in possession of the ball. Once the ball was in midfield, it was passed about until there was an opportunity to shoot or it was passed into the box and knocked into the goal. While I watched Isledon Wolves, they had scored three goals, quickly and efficiently. I knew Canaan would fit right into this system, and I looked forward to meeting Adrian at training.

The training session was at Mount Carmel school. When we got there, Adrian was starting his warm-up and stretching. I introduced myself and told him about Canaan.

About halfway through the session, Adrian turned to me and smiled. I smiled back, and I knew he wanted Canaan to be a part of his team. We got talking and Adrian and I hit it off straight away. He talked about his philosophy, and it was amazing how we believed a lot of the same things. I told him how I had monitored Canaan's development and wanted to make sure he was improving year by year. I felt he could help take him to another level. I do believe there have been three defining moments in Canaan's development: finding Brazilian Soccer School, meeting Adrian, and another moment I will tell you about later in the book.

Adrian felt the coaching in England was shockingly bad. He felt too many coaches believed in the long ball philosophy, and this was why kids were not developing.

He saw himself as an unorthodox coach because he didn't do the traditional long ball philosophy; which tells you something about England's coaching standards. Adrian had been a coach for over fifteen years and was passionate about coaching. He wanted high standards. Winning was important to him, but more important was how the team played and the manner of how the team won. He was a passionate guy and sometimes could lose it and swear at the sidelines, but I didn't mind. It was always about what was best for the kids' development, which is what you want from a coach, to tell you straight and not bullshit you. I have seen Adrian take on a new player other coaches have told him not to bother with because they are no good. He has always said if a player is coachable and willing to listen, he will work with them and develop them. I have seen him take players on and give them confidence and develop them time and time again. Adrian told me Canaan needed to work on his fitness and improve his work rate, but he was happy with the rest of his game. Canaan was at a decent level of fitness, but Adrian played a high-pressing game, and he liked to get his players to a high level of fitness. He told me there was a tournament coming up and he wanted me to bring Canaan along.

Canaan has been to countless trials and tournaments at junior clubs. I remember when we attended a South End FC trial and they were interested in Canaan, but we did it for the experience. We would hear about football events and turn up. Canaan has no problem turning up to a new team and getting straight into it because we have joined different teams and moved about, which has helped him with his confidence. When he joins a new team, he gets right down to business. Canaan spoke with his mum because he wanted her to up his fitness training; she is a fitness instructor.

He had been doing a little bit, but he wanted to take it more seriously. His mum put him on a fitness schedule and Canaan had no problem sticking to it.

Adrian played a high-pressing game; all his players were fit. Whenever his team lost the ball, they won it back quickly and went back to their passing game. Often they beat teams before they had even scored a goal. The other team spent their time chasing the ball, and you could see a demoralised look on the faces of the players. Isledon Wolves would drain the life from the opposite team and then score goals for fun. The summer tournaments were excellent for kids' development. They were intense, and you never had much time to score goals. I think it was five or ten minutes each way. The games were played at a blistering pace. You had to think fast and get the ball under control as quickly as possible. The pitches were not big; you would be closed down immediately and could lose the ball if you dwelled on it. Canaan loved them, and they always brought the best out of him. These tournaments are played on grass, which is where Canaan is at his most comfortable. His turns and quick feet can have such a devastating effect on defenders when he is playing on grass. Canaan made his debut for Adrian, and my memory is a bit hazy: all I remember was it poured down with rain and Canaan did his thing. He was on fire with his dribbling, and the rain gave him more of an advantage. The defenders were slipping and dropping all over the place.

'That boy is quality; are we signing him?'

It was nice to hear this from his potential new teammates. Adrian told them they would be signing him. Isledon Wolves ended up getting to the semi-finals and got knocked out on penalties. It felt like the only way they were going to lose. They were a strong team, with a strong goalkeeper, strong defence, and strong midfield. They were probably the weakest in attack, but they had signed Canaan, and we were looking forward to next season.

PRE-SEASON TRAINING

Adrian's training was intense. His fitness training was the best we had come across. He would do dynamic and agility training. A lot of players trialling out and hoping to get into the team ended up leaving. Isledon Wolves started to get a reputation as a hard team to play for. Adrian didn't mince his words, and he told you straight what he thought about your kid and how good he was and what he needed to work on. Some parents don't want to hear anything bad about their kids and struggle to take criticism. I felt comfortable with Adrian voicing his thoughts to me. I could see it was all coming from a place where he wanted the players to develop and get better. I also knew Canaan was in good hands, making me relax and not have to scrutinise everything. He would drill them on passing and keeping the ball, over and over. He would make players do press-ups if they gave away the ball needlessly. He wanted the players to express themselves and to be productive with the ball, whether a long pass or taking on a player, not kicking the ball aimlessly and hoping. He knew you might lose the ball when attempting a pass or trying to take on a player, but he wanted to see how you reacted if you lost the ball.

Canaan's work rate improved dramatically under Adrian, his fitness also. As a dad, this is all I wanted from Canaan's coach. Identify areas which need work and bring them up to me. I brought things up to him too that I felt needed work, and Adrian liked that. It was a relationship, not him just telling me what he thought was best. Some coaches are so focused on winning and tactics that they couldn't even tell you what areas of your kid's game need to be worked on. It was amazing how quickly Adrian could assess a new player, and he wasn't just looking for pace and power.

In England, we like to focus on getting the ball long or getting the ball wide and crossing it into the box for someone to get ahead on it, and because many of the pro clubs believe in this philosophy, it filters all the way down to grassroots football, where you have coaches only wanting the biggest kids or the fastest kids. Scouts are only looking for the biggest or fastest kids. There is no need for technical players. Technical players don't do well in a long ball game, but they thrive in a passing game where there are lots of touches of the ball, which is intricate football. What is England's philosophy? I couldn't tell you because I don't know. I can tell you Spain's philosophy. Spain plays a passing game and has dominated international football. The players they develop are geared to one day playing in the national team. The majority of the Spanish league are Spanish players.

In England, players are developed to play in the Premiership, not for the national team. The national team has no identity. If England doesn't do well, the manager is sacked and a new manager is brought in. There is no philosophy, no style, and no direction. The style of England becomes a product of whatever manager is brought in. I would like to see England put a philosophy in place that does not change no matter how many times the manager changes. The manager should fit the philosophy of England and not the other way around. I would also like to see England be more involved in scouting players that fit the philosophy of England, as opposed to England relying on pro clubs to bring players through for them. With academies having more foreign players and less English players, there could be less and less English players coming through.

The new season was around the corner and Canaan was pumped. One dad had told me about Arsenal Kicks, which was a project set up to bring football into the local community. Canaan loved it. It was training the Arsenal way: lots of touches of the ball, lots of ball work, and kids were encouraged to express themselves with the ball. They would play small-sided football matches, where there was not a lot of time and space on the ball and you could see the kids developing. One of the coaches, called Matt, liked Canaan; he was invited down to Arsenal Development, which was in Highgate School. There were lots of kids in different age groups from seven up to fourteen, all being coached the Arsenal way and it was nice to see kids developing technically.

This was the place I met Ryan, the third defining moment of Canaan's development. Ryan was not a loud guy; he was the quiet, confident type and was knowledgeable when it came to his football. I simply love this guy. We had similar beliefs when it came to our philosophy on football and kids' development in football. Ryan would tell you how it is and not bullshit you. He and Adrian were similar. I do think all good coaches will tell you how it is and not bullshit you. There is nothing worse than a coach constantly over-praising. There is nothing wrong with praising your players, but it has to be moderate. I know some excellent coaches who are not coaching anymore, and I think it is a tragedy for grassroots football. All because they were not getting the help they needed. They simply got fed up and quit.

I would like to give a tribute to Richard who ran the Brazilian Soccer School in Barnet and who helped with the development of Canaan and was developing some fantastic technical players. He was another coach who got fed up with the whole mentality of coaches at grassroots level. He told me of the arguments he would have with coaches that had their UEFA 'B' licence.

Over and over, he would explain to coaches it is about development and not how many matches you win. He told me because he never had his UEFA 'B' licence, he was not considered a good coach and was treated like he didn't know what he was doing. I don't care what badges or licences you have got. What I care about are your style and philosophy and whether you love coaching and are passionate about it.

The new season was here, and Canaan was in no mood to mess about. He had been worked on his fitness in the break and from Adrian's pre-season training, and you could see the results Canaan was getting. Canaan established himself quickly at Isledon Wolves. Canaan was scoring goals for fun and Isledon Wolves were top of the league. During one game, Canaan scored two goals; he'd absolutely terrorised the opposing team. At the end of the match, the opposing coaches came and shook Canaan's hand and asked him his name. The owner of Isledon Wolves came over to Canaan.

He gave Canaan tickets to an Arsenal FC football match. Canaan was over the moon, and he and I went and watched Arsenal versus Bolton.

During the first six months of Canaan playing for Isledon Wolves, he played at a high level and established himself as the main striker. He was creating and scoring goals. Canaan was playing a match for Isledon Wolves and he was terrorising like he does. When he came off, he told me about a little pain in his knee. He hadn't had any bad tackles against him. I told him if it got any worse while he was playing, to let Adrian know to take him off. The pain never came back, and he was able to finish the match. Isledon Wolves went on to win the match comfortably. The pain in the knee went away and I never thought anything of it. Then he was playing a match and disaster struck. Canaan was dribbling with the ball and, all of a sudden, he pulled up and stopped. He then started limping. I was a bit confused because no one was near him when it happened. Adrian took him off, and I went and spoke to him. Canaan told me he got an incredible pain in his knee. I told Adrian I was taking him home, and we left. I was not too sure what was going on, but we iced his knee and kept it elevated. The next day, the pain was still at the same level, so we took him to the doctors and were sent to the hospital for an MRI scan. We had to wait a few weeks for the scan to come back. In the meantime, Canaan was told no football. It was the first time Canaan had an injury where he was out. He was not happy, and it hit him hard. But this is what comes with being a footballer.

When the scan came back, Canaan was diagnosed with Sinding-Larsen-Johansson syndrome. SLJ, also known as Sinding-Larsen-Johansson disease, is a painful knee condition that most commonly affects teens during periods of rapid growth. Your kneecap is connected to your shinbone by the patellar tendon. When you're still growing, the tendon attaches to a growth plate at the bottom of the kneecap. Repetitive stress on the patellar tendon can cause this growth plate to become irritated and inflamed. SLJ is not a problem if identified and dealt with immediately-with a physical rehabilitation program to strengthen the muscles of the leg and increase their flexibility and range of motion.

In professional football, if a player gets injured, they have physios on standby to attend to the player. The player is sent for scans, and then the player is given a rehabilitation program as well as a time when he can come back to full training. At grassroots level, if a player gets injured, he is told to sit on the sidelines. The coach might have a word with him, but he is generally focused on the team and how the team is playing. Coaches have to know first aid, but I don't know if it is enough; yet I don't expect a coach to be a physio. Sometimes an ambulance is at matches. With all the NHS cuts, it's understandable an ambulance can't be at all the matches. I am much happier when an ambulance is on standby. When Canaan has any problems with his body, I treat him how the professional clubs treat their players. I want to get to the root of any problems. I want to highlight this for other parents as sometimes your kid may have an injury and you may brush it off, thinking it will get better on its own. Most injuries do. But the injury Canaan had was to do with his growth, and there could have been long-term complications if I did not act decisively and seek professional help.

I remember when I was watching an under tens match and one of the players fell awkwardly onto his wrist. The coach hauled him off and sat him down on the sidelines. He was crying, and you could see he was in pain. He tried to get the coach's attention, but the coach was more interested in what was going on in the match. The boy sat down with tears in his eyes for about twenty minutes until the match finished. I don't know where the boy's parents were. I don't think they were at the match.

Even once the match ended, the coach still had not tended to the boy. When he did finally acknowledge the boy, he told him, 'Don't cry, this is a man's game.' The next time I saw that boy, he had his arm in a cast, and it turned out he had fractured his wrist. If Canaan had been in that much pain, I would have immediately taken him to the hospital. There have been times when a ball has hit him in the face and he has felt dizzy and I have taken him there. The professional clubs are overly precautious when it comes to their players. I don't know if it is because of that player's value to the club or the player's health. Either way, they act decisively, and the player is assessed by the club's physio and sent away for scans. I believe I need to act the same way when it comes to Canaan. After all, he is important to me, and my kids are the most valuable people in my life. I want parents to be aware of these things and be more involved with their kid's development. I know parents have commitments and you might not want to spend your evening out watching a football match in the cold and rain, but believe me, they will appreciate it.

A DIFFICULT TIME

Canaan was told to stop all activities. I had to write him a note for school as it was not just football but all physical activities. This wasn't a good time for Canaan; keeping his morale up was difficult. We didn't have a time for when he would be back, and that stressed him out. I kept going over the points that this is part of being a footballer and encouraged him not to take it as a negative, but to take it as a positive and enjoy his break. My talking to him helped, but he missed football. It was difficult for him. When we met up with the physios, Canaan was given stretching exercises and strengthening exercises. It took about two months for the exercises to have an effect, and he slowly started light football training. As soon as he started to up the intensity of training, he started to get the same pain again but in the other knee. This time, we were ready. He stopped all training and continued his stretching and strengthening exercises on the other knee. It took another two months for his knees to finally clear up and for him to return to full training. By the time Canaan came back, the season was almost over and Isledon Wolves had won the league. Canaan was happy his team had won, but he wanted to be more involved. At the beginning of the season, Canaan was vital to Isledon Wolves' title challenge and, even though the team won, he never got to contribute to the second half of the season. Isledon Wolves would be going into the Harrow League as well as Camden and Islington League and Islington Cup.

Isledon Wolves would be entering into some summer tournaments, and Canaan was excited. He loved them, quick-paced on grass, and he couldn't wait. The first tournament they would be going to was the Edmonton tournament. When Canaan had a tournament, his mum and I would make a day of it. It was a nice day out. We would make sandwiches, have lots of snacks and drinks. On this particular day, the sun was beaming. It was hot. We had drinks we had frozen the night before. Canaan was raring to go, and he couldn't wait for the matches to kick off. For the early group stages, Isledon Wolves had no problems getting through; they were too good. Canaan was playing well, but I could tell he had not played football for a while. His touch was off, and he was playing it a bit safe and not taking on players. Canaan was focused on making sure he got game time; he didn't want to make any mistakes.

Once Isledon Wolves had completed their final group game, they qualified at the top of the group and were into the knockout stage. There was a little intermission where the knock out schedule was sorted out. While this was going on, I had a little chat with Canaan. I told him to relax and have fun.

Canaan always has his best games when he is taking on players and creating. We got the new schedule and the games started to kick off. We had to move all our stuff because we were on a new pitch. Isledon Wolves kicked off their first knockout match, Canaan started to relax, and he began trying his skills. He gained more confidence and was now taking on more players and dribbling more. The goals started to come, and Isledon easily disposed of the opposing team and were through to the quarterfinals. Adrian never started Canaan in the quarterfinals. Isledon Wolves started the match strong. They created chance after chance, but the ball would not go into the goal.

Then Isledon Wolves' intensity started to go down a bit. You could see the players getting a bit tired. They had a lapse in concentration, and the opposing team scored a goal. Half time came, and Adrian told the players they had been unlucky and to keep going and the goals would come. Isledon Wolves were such a quality team it was always a surprise when they were losing, but you always felt they could score a goal anytime. Adrian started Canaan in the second half, and he came on and had an immediate impact. The opposing team was not prepared for a player to pick up the ball and drive at them. He began to destabilize the opposing team's defence. The opposition began to panic when Canaan had the ball and they started to lose their shape. One move Canaan did was to draw the defender to him while facing towards his own goal and then drag the ball through his own legs. Now he faced the opposing goal. He then drove down the wing and laid the ball off to his teammate, who then took a shot, which was saved by the goalkeeper and pushed out for a corner. From the resulting corner, the ball was crossed low into the box and Canaan poked it into the goal. He had got the equalising goal. I felt happy for him and was a proud father. The move he had done was called Junior, also known as a Cruyff turn. He had learnt the turn at Brazilian Soccer School, and it was a beautiful turn which was executed to perfection. It was one thing to do that turn in training, but to do it in a competitive match takes confidence and trust in your coach to allow you to express yourself.

The match had ended 1-1 and was forced into penalties; you could see penalties made the players nervous. Canaan loved taking penalties. He was always one of the first to put his hand up to take one. He never changes the way he takes them, low bottom corner, low bottom corner. Canaan stepped up and confidently put the ball into the bottom corner, leaving no chance for the opposing goalie. The penalties continued on till sudden death; the first person to miss with the other team scoring and it would be over. The opposing player stepped up. He shot, and it was a fantastic save. Isledon Wolves' goalie was an excellent goalkeeper.

Adrian had developed him into a fine goalkeeper, and it shows you what a top coach Adrian was. In all my years of working with different coaches, Ryan, Adrian, Mike, and Warren were the only coaches that would do one-on-one sessions with the goalkeeper. They gave the goalkeepers different drills to do from the rest of the team. It should be common sense, shouldn't it? Well, believe it or not, a lot of coaches tell the goalkeepers to join in the drills the rest of the team are doing. Many coaches don't know how to develop a kid that wants to be a goalkeeper. As a parent, if your kid wants to be a goalkeeper, it is imperative you talk to the coach and find out about his or her goalkeeping training and watch the coaching sessions to see if the goalkeepers are being developed correctly. As a coaching session comes to an end, most coaches will play a match, and you don't want the only development your kid gets to be playing in the match at the end.

All Isledon Wolves had to do was score this last penalty and they would be through to the semi-finals. The player stepped up and blasted it home. There was cheering, shouting, and hugging. Adrian wanted to calm the team down. He reminded them we still had two games to go, and it quickly brought them back to reality. Isledon Wolves started the semi-final with a bang. They were moving the ball around quickly and sharply. The two touch and three touch football were exhilarating. Sometimes I could feel sorry for the opposing team when Isledon Wolves were playing like this. It didn't seem fair. You could see the life and spirit drain from the players when they spent most of their time chasing the ball.

Sometimes when it took the opposing team long to get the ball back, they ended up giving it back to Isledon Wolves. When Isledon Wolves didn't have the ball, they would press and harry the opposition, forcing them to lose the ball and give it right back to Isledon Wolves; they would start the process again and begin passing the ball around, letting the other team do all the chasing. The teams which did well against Isledon Wolves were the teams that pressed intensely and never gave the Isledon players time on the ball. Pressing at high intensity will test the team's fitness levels and, unfortunately, most under twelves junior clubs are not fit. Playing possession football was as important to Adrian as being fit. One of the reasons a lot of players were put off playing for Isledon Wolves was Adrian's reputation with his fitness training. New players would come, and they would leave, never to be seen again.

Isledon Wolves were three up within a matter of minutes. Adrian had started Canaan this game and he carried on where he had left off in the last match. Even though Adrian and I were close, he never gave Canaan any special treatment. Adrian would drop Canaan for different reasons. Sometimes it was because he was not working hard enough, and sometimes he felt he looked tired. Canaan played the majority of games. I never took it to heart because I totally trusted in Adrian, a hard place to get to with the coach of your kid.

Isledon Wolves had made it to the final, Canaan's first final. The team they were playing was a good team, organised, and they were trying to play possession football. This was going to be a tough match. Adrian was cool and calm as always. The parents were a nervous wreck, including me. The players didn't have long to wait; they kicked off the match within ten minutes. It was the Isledon Wolves' players and the opposing players left knocking the ball about. The place where the tournament was being held, by this time, was almost empty as a lot of people had gone home. It felt a bit weird being there with hardly anyone there. The match kicked off and Isledon Wolves were straight at the opposing team from the whistle. The opposing coach had done his homework or had watched some of our games, because he was drilling his team to keep their shape and stay well organised. Also, he was attempting to hit Isledon Wolves on the counter attack. Isledon Wolves couldn't create many goal-scoring opportunities against this team. They were not willing to come out and engage Isledon Wolves. Isledon Wolves had played teams like this before, which were well organised, but they would always end up losing shape and discipline, but not this team. They stuck to the coach's game plan. The ref blew the whistle for full time, and it was going to be straight into penalties, no extra time. The players had a ten-minute break before it was time to start penalties. This was a tense time. None of the players wanted to leave as losers.

Growing up, I have always heard the saying 'Winning is not as important as taking part'. Now the football players playing at the highest level will tell you that is bullshit. At the highest level, winning is the most important thing. Winning can decide how long a career you can have. If you are losing all the time, your career is going to be short. If you are not performing, your career is going to be short. These are the facts. The problems arise at grassroots football, where development and winning get blurred. Should winning be important to an under eights or under nines? Or should it be about development and fun? In my opinion, it should be about fun and development until they are at least thirteen. Once winning becomes important, it also adds pressure to perform and pressure to win.

The ref blew his whistle to start the penalties. The Isledon Wolves' goalie was on fire. He was saving everything. It all came down to this last penalty; if we scored we won, but if we didn't, the penalties would continue.

Isledon Wolves had been playing good football all tournament, and the player stepping up to take the penalty knew this. He knew Adrian was already a satisfied coach. He was stepping up to take the penalty all relaxed and blasted it into the bottom corner. Isledon Wolves had won the Edmonton tournament. There was cheering and shouting from the parents. The players went over to the opposing team and shook their hands and consoled them. No one likes to lose, but it must not be made a big deal at grassroots level; it still should be fun. The Isledon Wolves' players had a ceremony where they were all handed individual trophies and a big one to Adrian. They then had their picture taken, which was printed in the *Islington Gazette*. I went and congratulated Adrian and also the Isledon Wolves team players. They all looked shattered, including Canaan. We packed up the entire picnic gear and congratulated everyone one more time and left to go home. Canaan was on a high, and I was happy for him to be playing football again after all the injuries.

IT ALL STARTS AGAIN

Canaan was going into his next season. He would now be going into under thirteens and his physique was starting to fill out. He was becoming tall. Canaan loved his food and did not mess about when it came to mealtime. Isledon Wolves' junior club started grass football from under thirteens. Canaan would be playing in the Harrow League and in the Camden and Islington League at Market Road and also in the Camden and Islington Cup and Harrow Cup. One of Canaan's teammates dropped out of the Camden and Islington and wanted to concentrate on the Harrow League. Canaan considered doing that but wanted to still play at Market Road. Also, Canaan had gotten over his injury problems but was not at the level he was before he got his injuries, so he wanted to play as much football as possible. This was the season where he started not to enjoy playing on AstroTurf. Canaan loved playing on grass but struggled to get his motivation up to playing on AstroTurf. Also, we started to realise that after a match on AstroTurf, his feet would be in much more pain and took longer to recover than a match on grass. When I spoke to a podiatrist about this problem, she told me playing football on AstroTurf is not good for the soles of your feet. She knew kids all over the country did it, but she recommended playing on grass as much as possible and avoiding AstroTurf. Canaan decided that he would not be playing in the Camden and Islington League next year. The pitches over at Market Road were over twenty years old. It was almost like playing on concrete pitches. Once Canaan had decided he would not be playing in the Camden and Islington League next year, it gave him extra motivation to win everything. He wanted to go out with a bang.

Canaan's form was inconsistent; even though he had gotten over his injury issues, he was not playing to the level he was capable of. Canaan was still scoring goals in the Harrow League. He was scoring a goal a game but struggled with the pace of the Camden and Islington League. His body was still going through changes and, although he had no problems with his knees, other areas of his body were tight. We also noticed he kept getting little niggles. We continued doing the stretches, and any new body part that started feeling tight, we would start doing stretches on that area. It was a frustrating period for him because he felt his body was letting him down. His touch and his sharpness were not back to the level they had been. He was struggling to get a consistent run of games for Isledon Wolves. Canaan missed many of the Market Road games because he needed time to recover. Sometimes there could be a Market Road game on the Friday and then a Harrow game on the Sunday. If he played in one, then normally he would miss the other one. Canaan wanted to focus more on Harrow. Also, because of these issues, Adrian wanted to use him sparingly, so he found himself not starting a lot of games and being used as an impact sub. From being a main player to becoming a fringe player because of his injuries was frustrating. Some of the fringe players, who were not getting into the team, were now getting a run of games in the team and doing well. It was difficult to keep his spirits up.

This is what I mean when I talked about parents being more involved and not seeing it as some hobby or fun but as maybe a way of life and a career. If Canaan had to deal with all these issues by himself, how would he have coped? He might have given it up. It's difficult enough having to self-motivate and then having to go through injuries on your own. The Harrow League was where Canaan enjoyed his best performances. His form was inconsistent, but he was still scoring goals consistently. He was not having the same level of influence as before, therefore making his assists go down. Also, he was taking longer to get into the game.

Having talks with Canaan helped with getting his confidence back. We went over to the park and worked on the areas of his game Canaan felt he was struggling with. He worked harder with his mum on his fitness. I then had an idea to record his stats while I watched his matches. This was important in helping Canaan get his form back. We would look at the stats of his game, and he could see which parts of his game had a low output. It was difficult to get accurate numbers as I was doing it from memory, but I would give him a general idea of his stats for the match.

Now, I am not trying to make parents feel like shit parents by telling you all the things I do for Canaan to help improve his football. I am trying to open parents' eyes. I am not expecting you to be me. I am over the top with Canaan's football, but I see it as an opportunity for him to have a career in something he loves. Becoming a footballer is difficult enough. It's a sport where only 1 percent of English academy players go on to play football for the first team. If I don't think and act like I believe, then how do I expect him to? I want to give him the best possible help and encouragement. I take his football as seriously as I take his education. His mum is the main motivator when it comes to his education and I am the main motivator when it comes to his football. It's a beautiful balance.

A lot of the Isledon Wolves players were being monitored by scouts. This annoyed Canaan as he was not able to perform at the top of his game during this period. Some of the scouts would come to the match and drink tea and chat with people. I wondered if they were even watching the match. Then you had the scouts that were totally focused on the match. I never knew if there were going to be scouts at the match beforehand, and I never knew what the scouts looked like. Scouts did not stand out. There would be whispers among the parents and someone would show you where the scout was. Adrian would sometimes know scouts would be at the match. He did not like telling the players when this happened; he didn't tell them before the match, only after. When he would tell them before the match, the players would become greedier with the ball. They would try different things they would not normally do. The players would not play their natural game.

Usually, when the season ended, Adrian went straight into training for the new season to get them ready for the summer tournaments. His lads had won the treble, and he wanted them to have a break before he started training. Canaan was not having a break. He was back working with his mum and continuing his stretches. Canaan's level of dedication would amaze me sometimes. But when you love what you are doing, it becomes easy. I have never had any problems with taking Canaan to training. Sometimes he has not looked up for it, then once he gets to training, he becomes a different person. He also had Adrian, who was one of the most dedicated coaches Canaan has worked with. If it was snowing and the players were still able to play on the pitch, Adrian was there. If Adrian was ill, he would still be there. I remember a time when Adrian had got into a car crash, not too serious, but he had hurt his back. He could barely walk, but there he was, providing training for the kids. It also made the kids more dedicated, and they knew how important training was to get selected for the match.

Training facilities must have been one of the most frustrating problems for Adrian. There was a point where the club got hit with cuts and lost their sponsorship. This meant they were unable to continue training in a school they were using; at this point, Adrian never had anywhere to train. Adrian had to train anywhere he could get free. We would train at Market Road when the pitches hadn't been booked, but we never knew when that was. Adrian could be starting to set up for training and we would have to leave because it was booked. Adrian would have to train at the side while the match was playing. The adults using the pitch were never happy with this and Adrian got into a few arguments. Adrian trained in a park that had more dog shit than grass. He also trained on a concrete pitch that was used by the local kids. The club did manage to book Market Road pitch for two hours once a week. Adrian liked to train twice a week, but the club could not help him with facilities for the other session; he was on his own. Adrian bounced around from place to place to get the other session in for the kids. He would come out of his house not knowing if he would have somewhere to train, but he would still do it for the kids. At one point, Adrian had a treble-winning team with nowhere to train.

A story has been in the media recently that the FA is going to invest a quarter of a billion pounds into grassroots football over the next four years. They have identified four key areas:

'Boosting Participation: Building on the increases in the boys and girls participation and growth in disability football, while delivering more varied formats of the game to address the drop in traditional 11v11 weekend football among adult males.'

'Developing better players: £4 million per year-including an annual £2 million investment from the government-will be invested in grassroots coaching. There will be a network of County

Coaches-tasked with improving and supporting coaching across grassroots football with club mentoring programmes. The extension of coach bursaries will get more women and people from diverse backgrounds into the profession and there will be a drive to get more top level grassroots coaches into the game.'

'Better training and facilities: The FA is committing £48million–directly through its funding of the Football Foundation as well as an investment in 100 new turf pitches and improvements to a further 2,000 as part of The FA's Pitch Improvement Plan. Further funds have also been dedicated to building 30 new football hubs across key cities–with a pilot scheme already underway in Sheffield–with the Government committed to providing £8m per year over five years to support The FA's contribution.'

'Football workforce: Football will become more representative of the communities it serves through inclusion initiatives. The FA is also rolling out technology to run the game more efficiently and create direct lines of communication with players across all grassroots leagues making football truly integrated.'

You can read the full article at www.thefa.com.

This is fantastic news that the FA will unveil this ambitious plan. My concern is where does their information about the issues on grassroots football come from? How close is the FA to grassroots football? This is a massive plan and I want the FA to get it right. I am a part of grassroots football; I have been for the last eight years. It has taken years for me to understand what I believe is a good coach and what is not. I have seen different styles of training and football that develop the kids differently. The FA wants to build 'on the increases in boys and girls participation and growth in disability football.' Will this only be for fun? Or will there be a chance for someone with a disability to have a career in football? They are 'delivering more varied formats of the game to address the drop in traditional 11 v 11 weekend football among adult males.' This issue is the least one I am concerned about. I am more concerned we keep growing the numbers of kids in their teens playing eleven vs. eleven football. When kids enter their teenage years, they start to have a lot more freedom and there are many more distractions. Football has helped to keep Canaan focused. He knows he has to make sure he is doing what he needs to do in school or it will affect his football. Football makes him watch his diet; he lives by the eighty-twenty rule, which means eighty percent of the time he eats healthy and twenty percent of the time he eats what he wants. He wants to keep fit and gain any extra advantage in his football. He can't be up late at night if he has a match or training the next day. As you can see, football has had a positive influence on Canaan's life. I see many teenagers who have given up football even though they used to love it, and I think this is more damaging for grassroots football than adult numbers falling.

The FA wants to invest money in developing better players. I am excited about this area of the strategy. 'There will be a network of County Coaches-tasked with improving and supporting coaching across grassroots football with club mentoring programmes.' I want to know what the FA defines as a good coach. If the county coaches are no good, then this strategy will fail. Lots of coaches that have all their badges sometimes think they know it all, and they get an ego.

'The FA is committing £48 million for better training and facilities.' Now, obviously this is fantastic from the FA, but one of the main complaints I hear from coaches is the cost of hiring out pitches. Therefore, I am going to assume these better facilities are not going to be free. A problem still exists. What's the point in having all these better training facilities if the coaches and junior clubs can't afford to use them? The cost of hiring a pitch can vary between eighty and ninety pounds for one hour. Now, if you want to put on a training session twice a week of two hours, it will cost you between three hundred and fifty or sixty pounds per week. While a lot of coaches would like to train for four hours a week, they are forced to settle for two hours a week. If the coaches are not able to spend a considerable amount of time working with the kids week in, week out, then how are the kids supposed to develop and get better? What is the point of improving the training and facilities if the coaches and junior clubs can't afford to use them? Also, many of the pitches are hired out to adults. Now, I know it needs to be equal and the pitches should be available to anyone, but the point of this ambitious plan is to improve grassroots football, creating better players and better coaching. If the coaches can't afford to hire the pitches or they can never get a pitch because they are booked up for leisure activities, how are we supposed to create better players and improve coaching? These are the issues I hear about at grassroots now, and I haven't seen anything in the ambitious plan to address these issues.

Another issue that has not come up in the plan is how much grassroots coaches are paid. It is below the minimum wage, and you can understand with all the costs the junior clubs have to pay-pitch hire, league entry, kits, summer tournaments, coaches, and award ceremonies-grassroots coaches have to do a lot for nothing. If they did not go the extra mile, I don't know how many junior clubs would survive. Most grassroots coaches are volunteers, and I think it is one of the reasons the standard of coaching is low. There is no incentive to be a grassroots coach. Why would top-level coaches stay working at grassroots level for low pay or no pay when they can go to a professional football club and get paid good money? I don't care how passionate you are about coaching, you still need to put food on the table and pay the bills, and the majority of grassroots coaches have another job which is their main job.

Becoming a coach feels like a hobby as opposed to feeling excited about having a career. A lot of the coaches I know that have stopped coaching felt there was no appreciation for what they were doing for grassroots football, and they came to realise it was not worth the hassle.

ANOTHER TOURNAMENT, ANOTHER CHALLENGE

Canaan was going into the under fourteens and looking more and more like an athlete. Adrian had started back training; he wanted to prepare the team for the summer tournaments. They would be going into the Edmonton tournament, the tournament they won a couple of years ago. Canaan was looking forward to the tournament as he missed last year's due to injury, but he was ready to go. His body was feeling much better and he had been working hard with his mum on his fitness. Adrian was going to pick his team for the tournament based on how the players were performing in training. Not all the players could go to the tournament because there were limited spaces. A week before the tournament in Adrian's last training session, Adrian told the players he would send out texts to whoever had been selected for the tournament. Canaan was quite confident he would make the team; he had no reason to believe he wouldn't.

Canaan was getting a bit anxious. It was only two days before the tournament and we had not received any text yet. Adrian and I were close, and I could have rung him to find out what was going on, but I didn't want to, as I didn't want to influence his decision in any way.

I rang Adrian the next day, and he explained to me it was a hard decision, but he wanted to go with someone else instead of Canaan. He felt Canaan was still not ready for the fast-paced summer tournament, and he was a bit worried he would bring Canaan along and he would have to end up sitting out, or be unable to perform to the levels he could because Canaan had not played much football lately. I told Adrian I accepted his decision and would let Canaan know.

Adrian had made his mind up and I was going to have to explain to Canaan he had not been selected. I was sitting on the sofa waiting for Canaan to get in from school, eating some food and feeling a bit anxious. I knew Canaan was looking forward to the Edmonton tournament. About a half hour later, Canaan came through the front door looking all weary. I sat him on the sofa and explained to him what Adrian had told me. Canaan was trying not to cry, but a tear trickled down his cheek. I gave him a hug and told him not to worry. He could carry on working with his mum until he was ready.

I sent Adrian a text because I wanted him to know what effect leaving Canaan out of the team had on him. Adrian felt like he had made a mistake and swapped one of the players out and put Canaan in. I told Canaan and he was overjoyed but felt like he had something to prove.

It was the day of the tournament and Canaan was pumped. He felt he had to remind Adrian and his teammates how good he was.

And remind them he did. He was immense from the first game to the last. Adrian couldn't believe how he was playing and was happy to have brought him along. Isledon Wolves were beating everybody, and Canaan was scoring goals for fun. Another one of the Isledon Wolves' players was also having a fantastic tournament, and it felt like a battle between him and Canaan to see who would finish as the top goal scorer. Isledon Wolves were blowing away all comers. Isledon Wolves got to another final; we couldn't believe it. Adrian had not expected too much because they had struggled the year before. He was hoping they could get to a semi-final, maybe a final. The final got underway, and I knew before the match Isledon Wolves were going to win. I saw it in the players' eyes and Canaan's eyes. There was no way they would get to the final and leave empty-handed. Canaan was in the mood and, when he's like that, he doesn't lose. Canaan picked up the ball from the halfway line; he beat one player, then he beat another, and then he slotted the ball into the bottom corner.

When Canaan is in full flow, he glides past players. His quick feet and change of direction make him a nightmare for defenders. *What a goal!* I thought. I had seen him do goals like that a couple of times, but as he has got older, those types of goals have been more frequent. The other Isledon player that had been playing fantastic got two goals in the final, and the final ended 3-0. The players and parents celebrated; this was the second time Isledon Wolves had won the Edmonton tournament.

There was a scout from Brentford FC who had been watching the final and was interested in the other player that was doing as well as Canaan. The scout had watched the whole final and saw Canaan score that amazing goal, but that did not pique his interest. All he cared about was the other player. Now, don't get me wrong, as I mentioned earlier, the boy was having an amazing tournament and playing excellently, but his attributes were power and pace. He was strong and quick, not with blistering pace but quick enough to be noticed. Canaan is more of the graceful type of player. His dribbling and close control are slick and smooth. When you see these things happen over and over, you feel the scouts are only looking for one type of player and if you don't fit the mould, then they are not interested. The scout not being interested in Canaan after his performance never bothered him. He was used to it now. 'I am not the type of player they like in England and I have to accept it.'

TRUSTING YOUR GRASSROOTS COACH

How do you put your complete and utter trust into a coach to develop your kid correctly when a lot of grassroots coaches are volunteers and part-time coaches? Canaan has been lucky to have worked with some excellent coaches over the years, but I have met some bad ones. The sad thing is they think they are brilliant coaches and don't want to be told anything. I have seen kids that have started out on similar level as Canaan and, where Canaan has gone on and progressed, these other kids have regressed. Some kids who I actually thought were better than Canaan are nowhere near the level Canaan is now.

Kevin Davies is a former professional football player with 446 Premier League appearances. He played with Southampton, Blackburn, and Bolton, while also representing his country at the age of thirty-three in 2010. While doing some research, I came across an article where Kevin was giving his experiences with his son. He explained that his son was playing for a local team and, although the manager was a nice guy, Kevin felt the manager knew nothing about football and asked the head of Bolton's Academy if his son could attend some training sessions. Within weeks, his son blossomed and improved technically by having an extra three hours quality coaching each week. Kevin also believed if he had taken one of his son's mates from the same team, there would have been a similar improvement in him.

Kevin Davies makes the point that I have been expressing through the book. What is going to happen to the development of those other kids that are at Kevin's son's local team? Not everybody has the contacts to talk to the head of Bolton's Academy. I know I don't. What I did know is that I wanted Canaan to be developed correctly, and I knew I had to be totally involved in his development for that to happen. If we had stuck with one coach all these years, Canaan would not be the player he is today. I have been lucky to work with some talented coaches along the way. Coaches who I believe could go and work for football academies, and if the opportunity came, I believe would. In the article, Kevin mentioned that Mr Dyke needs to make coaching courses more affordable and accessible. Then we could get more high-quality coaches, but I don't see the incentive for high-quality coaches to coach at grassroots level. It's one of the reasons why there are a lot of volunteers and part-time coaches at grassroots level. The people that work at grassroots are generally good people that want to give back to the community, but coaching is not their ambition. If you want to have a career as a coach, why would you stay coaching at grassroots level?

Kevin had to ask Bolton to help because the standard of coaching at his local team was not good enough. This is one of the major problems I see at junior clubs. Kids that are picked up early by an academy have every possibility of getting the correct coaching and development. They are already on a stage to showcase their talent. If it doesn't work out with that club in particular, then because of the stage they are at, it is still possible to get picked up by another club. The other clubs will know that kid has been in the academy from a young age and his development will be of a certain level. The problems arise when kids don't get picked up by academies and are relying on grassroots coaches for their development. By the time these kids get into their teens, they are so far behind, development-wise, that no academies want them. I see kids at junior clubs year after year not improving, not progressing because of unplanned and little-prepared sessions. Sometimes the sessions seemed good because the coaches worked on lots of different attributes, i.e. shooting and passing, but with no reference to the real game. One of the things that made Adrian such a good coach was he knew how he wanted his team to play and develop. His coaching sessions were built around his beliefs, and he learnt what training would be most effective in getting his message across. He would do the same session over and over until it became natural for the players and transferred to the matches. Adrian never chased trophies; he chased development and that is why he won everything at grassroots.

How many junior clubs are providing high-quality coaching?

Data provided by the UEFA coaching convention statistics show that England has 1,395 coaches holding UEFA's A and pro-qualification badges. Now, compare this to our European neighbours: Germany has 6,937, Italy has 2,281, France has 3,308, and Spain has 15,423. When you look at the statistics, England are trailing behind our European neighbours, and when you think among France, Germany, Spain, and Italy, they have provided eleven out of sixteen participants in the World Cup and European championship finals since 1998.

Although the numbers are poor, especially compared to Spain's numbers, Nick Levett, the FA National Development Manager for Youth Football, disagrees with the numbers. Nick Levett explains on audio that when the UEFA coaching convention was formed, countries like Spain, Germany, and France gave every qualified coach a UEFA B licence since the 1970s. England as a nation did not want to do that and decided that coaches would have to go through the UEFA qualification. Nick Levett does not believe that the statistics actually reflect the current licenced coaches. In grassroots football, I don't believe it matters how many coaches there are with their UEFA A or B licence. Coaches don't want to be at junior clubs working with under eights and nines, they want to be working with older boys or in academies. Can you blame them? Poor facilities and aggressive parents that don't want to listen to the coach when the coach might have something valuable to tell them about their kid's development. Grassroots coaches don't get respect. Once you're a coach that works for a pro club academy, you get a different attitude from parents.

Increasing facilities and also improving the qualified coaches can only benefit grassroots football, but with unqualified volunteers and a majority of parents stepping up to coach at grassroots, this is where I feel the damage is being done. It is harming our football future. It annoys me that football is England's most popular sport, but we have unqualified volunteers in charge of long-term development in kids. To be fair on the volunteers, I am not upset with them, we obviously need them. It seems normal to turn up to training and it's another kid's parent taking control of the training session. Parents would not feel the same way if a volunteer was teaching their kid how to play tennis or how to swim, but in football, it's okay. Until we decide that it's not okay for volunteers to be responsible for the bloodline of English football, we will continue to get hoof-and-run games with unstructured training sessions.

The England national team does not stop being criticised for their performances at major tournaments. There is enormous pressure on the England team to do well, but the coaching at grassroots is a mess. Kids should be given the best opportunity to have a career in football and, if their development is being handled correctly, they will. Kids getting the opportunity is another issue altogether, and I will talk about that later in the book. Former under twenty-one coach Stuart Pearce has been vocal that the England under twenty-ones team has not won anything since 1984 and England's last major trophy was winning the World Cup in 1966, before I was born. England has never won the European football championship, and their best performance in the World Cup since they won it is a semi-final appearance in 1990. England's best performance in the European football championship is a semi-final appearance in 1968 and 1996.

Junior clubs need to be developing kids to academy level, or they need to be improving year by year. I don't think some parents realise how badly their kid is being developed. Parents will be told that a coach has all his qualifications and has been CRB checked (Criminal Records Bureau), and that is usually enough to satisfy the parents. If the coaches' main focus is winning and not player development, that's when the problems arise. Greg Dyke, the FA's chairman, set up a commission which has ex-international Rio Ferdinand and Danny Mills included. I am happy to see ex-footballers included. I can relate more to a footballer than I can to a board member in a suit. Especially with Rio Ferdinand. I grew up in Peckham too, and he knows how hard it is to grow up in an area like that and make something of yourself. I grew up on Camden Estate, Sumner Road, which had three gangs close to where I lived, and I was living behind the notorious Peckham frontline. Sometimes I couldn't go to the shop because it was taped off for a stabbing or murder.

Canaan was playing for an under sixteens semi-pro team. He established himself quite quickly and was an important player for the team. The coach had got to know Canaan and understood his game; he wanted to improve on it and add to him to make him a better player. Now, most recently, a new coach had come into the setup; his qualifications were higher than the current coach. He had all his level 1-3 qualifications and missed out on his UEFA B by four points. The first training session that the coach took was definitely an improvement on the current coach. His drills were structured and organised with a clear focus on what he wanted from the players. Sounds good, right?

Well, it was to a point; the problem is that his training focused on passing and overlapping runs. The training was all geared to scoring goals, not on individuals expressing themselves and improving individually. During a training match, Canaan beat two defenders and was through on goal. When this happened, the coach stopped the match.

He told Canaan that his teammate was in space and he should have passed the ball. Canaan didn't pass the ball; does that mean he was wrong? The pass was an option, and Canaan believes in his ability to beat other players. During training, the new coach told the players that unless they are two nil up in a game, then no dribbling. Coaches like this are destroying grassroots football. Once again, all this coach cared about was winning, not player development, and at grassroots level, player development should be priority. If Canaan had beat two players in Spain or Brazil, he would be celebrated, not condemned. I don't think it's a coincidence that of the top football players in the world, none of them are English. When was the last time Barcelona FC or Real Madrid FC paid a big money transfer fee for an English player?

FA's level 1 preaches that the golden years of learning are when kids are eight to twelve years old. I am a strong believer that technical development is all that should be taught to kids at these ages. It's not about producing mediocre or above average players. It should be about producing high-quality top players. To produce elite players, we need to have elite coaches. A coach that completes his UEFA A or B does not guarantee that he will develop top players. If his priority is to win and not develop kids, then it does not matter what qualification he has. I would like to see a more technical, possession-based game as mandatory at grassroots level, especially between the ages of eight to twelve. In my experience, too many times I see coaches wanting the biggest and strongest kids to bully other teams into submission. Only some junior clubs have an ethos and philosophy about player development and want to see possession-based football and kids developing technically through all age groups, but for the majority of junior clubs, the style of football and player development is left up to the coach. Now, if you have part-time coaches or volunteers in charge of football style and player development, working with kids from a young age, sometimes for years, what type of players will be developed?

FULLY FIT AND INJURY FREE

After an excellent tournament ending in Isledon Wolves being champions again, Canaan was looking forward to playing consistently and having a run of games. Together, we had decided that he would pull out of the Camden and Islington League and focus on the Harrow League. Canaan did not want to play on AstroTurf anymore. He wanted to focus on playing on grass. On AstroTurf, there was no offside and under fourteens was seven-a-side. For Canaan to develop the timing of his runs and beat the offside trap, he needed to play eleven-a-side grass football. Also, he preferred to play on grass in football boots.

The matches were coming thick and fast. Isledon Wolves were in the Harrow League and Harrow Cup. Adrian's possession-style-based football was too much for the opposing teams. Isledon Wolves had blown away all comers last year in Harrow League Division Three; for the new season, Isledon Wolves had been pushed up to Division One. Adrian was warned that he wouldn't have it his own way and it would be much harder and tougher in Division One. Adrian wasn't bothered; he was told the same thing when he first joined the Harrow League. Adrian knew he had created a quality team and believed that his team could have joined a higher league in the first place. It would take a good team to beat his team. Division One was a lot harder than Division Three. Teams were more organised, but the majority of the teams were using the formation 4-4-2 and kicking the ball long and chasing it. Isledon Wolves kept the ball on the ground. They played football from out the back, goalkeeper to defenders, midfield to strikers. The players had been playing this way since they were under tens, before Canaan had joined Isledon Wolves. All the players were comfortable on the ball and didn't want to kick the ball long, even when under pressure from an opposing player. The players would rather try and pass the ball to a teammate. Whether it was the goalkeeper under pressure or a defender, the players were always encouraged to try and find a teammate. Did the players make mistakes sometimes? Absolutely, but since it was the way Adrian wanted to play, he accepted that mistakes might happen. Adrian also used different formations, not the standard 4-4-2 formation. He liked to use 4-3-3 or 4-4-1-1.

Isledon Wolves were making a name for themselves in the Harrow League. Scouts from different pro clubs would come and see Isledon Wolves play. A lot was being said about Isledon Wolves. The level they were playing at was high, and it started to have an effect on the other teams in the league. Isledon

Wolves were scoring double figures in goals against some of the teams in the league, but not as much as the teams in Division Three. Some of the games were a lot closer. The other teams started to not turn up to the matches. They preferred to accept a loss for not turning up, which would only be a three-goal deficient. Teams not turning up were one problem. Another big problem was the pitches. Canaan and I would always be nervous if it had been raining a couple of days before the match. Sometimes we could turn up to the match and it was a mud pit. I would be sure that the referee would call it off, but the referee would be put under pressure by the parents, players, and coaches. Isledon Wolves struggled to play possession football when the pitch was mainly mud. The football would not roll, and the players would get stuck in the mud. Adrian would use the opportunity to make the players do long passing; not aimless long balls, but long passing. Adrian could get to develop another aspect of the players' development.

Another issue that would cause arguments amongst coaches and parents was the need for linesmen. Offside decisions, in my opinion, cause the most heated arguments I have seen at grassroots matches. A parent from each team volunteers to run the line, and it is up to the parents to flag a player offside or not. The parents can then become the target for other parents' and coaches' frustration. I did volunteer to run the line for a few months and, after a while of running the line, I decided to refuse to do it anymore. It felt like I was arguing every week with parents from the opposite team and sometimes with Adrian and parents from my own team. I understand how frustrated Adrian got with decisions not going his way. I tried to be fair when running the line and not cheat, but it was difficult, especially when the parents from the other teams didn't have the same ethics.

The FA wants to improve the number of 3G Astro pitches available, but I never hear how they can improve the grass pitches. Grass football gives kids the experience of playing in football boots and getting the feel of playing football on grass. If a career in football is going to happen, it will be on grass, not AstroTurf.

Canaan was having a good season. He was averaging a goal a game, but good is not good enough for Canaan; he was not hitting the levels that he wanted to hit. Canaan's consistency had been up and down. I couldn't put my finger on why, but I was happy that he was getting game time on a consistent basis. Isledon Wolves were playing well and were top of the league. Isledon Wolves were doing equally as well in the Camden and Islington League and Cup. They were on course to repeat the treble again. Problems started to arise when pro club scouts began to show an interest in particular players. When scouts came to the matches and the players knew, the players would try to impress and hold on to the ball for longer than necessary and not play their normal game. It got to the point that Adrian stopped telling the players if scouts were at the matches and told the scouts to come in normal clothes. Isledon Wolves never played well when the players knew scouts were watching. Once players started trialling with pro clubs, that's when the problems started.

With Isledon Wolves losing one of their best players, Canaan felt he had to step up his game. Canaan's form had been inconsistent. He would be the first person to admit that. Canaan was still scoring goals consistently, but he was going missing in games for long periods. The first game without the player that left was a tense affair for Canaan. Isledon Wolves were playing one of the other top teams in the league, the only team to beat Isledon Wolves in the season. Many expectations were put on Canaan's shoulders because of the other player leaving. Adrian played Canaan as a striker for most of his time at Isledon Wolves. Canaan had performed the role excellently, but he was starting to not enjoy it and felt he had better games as a provider or playmaker. He didn't like to wait around for supply and also enjoyed battling and winning the ball.

It is important to have a relationship with the coach.

I brought up the concerns to Adrian, and he agreed that we could try and play him more as a playmaker. Adrian always encouraged parents to talk to him as long as the parents were objective and not biased, which parents struggle with. Adrian wanted the best for Canaan and the other kids, and I felt that about him from the first moment I met him. It was the day of the match and Canaan had his game face on. The team they were playing were not a technical team, but they were a team of battlers, and Isledon Wolves lost to them in a previous match because they never matched them, they never let Isledon Wolves get their possession game going. This was a grudge match for Isledon Wolves and everybody connected with Isledon Wolves. The match kicked off and Canaan was in no mood to mess about. The pressure was on him with Isledon Wolves losing one of their star players. Canaan seems to always perform better when he is under pressure. Sometimes we have had some heated discussions about his game when he is too much in his comfort zone and not pushing himself, but in general, he is self-motivated, and he has been since he was a young boy.

Canaan was playing well. Adrian was playing the formation 4-3-3 and Canaan was left of the front 3 attack. The first half of the game came to an end for half-time. The score was 0 - 0 and both teams were playing well and had chances to score. The referee blew the whistle and got the second half underway. Adrian had decided to move Canaan from left of attack to central. Canaan loved this move by Adrian; he began to drop deeper and was finding space between the opponent's midfield and defence. He started to cause havoc to the opponent's defence with his dribbling and passing. Canaan was beginning to thrive, and I was starting to see his levels rise. Canaan was enjoying being a playmaker. Isledon Wolves scored two goals in quick succession and Canaan provided both. Two more goals for Isledon Wolves and, again, Canaan was involved in both. Canaan continued to create chance after chance for his teammates with through balls and his crossing. The final score ended 4-1 but Isledon Wolves should have won by a lot more. Canaan was given man of the match.

Adrian felt Isledon Wolves would struggle today. Isledon Wolves went on and finished top of the Harrow League and were crowned champions. The players had won everything, and the attendance at training had been dropping all season. All we have now are the memories of a great team and a great coach. Isledon Wolves folded, and coaches were contacting Adrian. It was not long before I got a recommendation from Adrian.

THE PRO ACADEMY ROUTE VS THE NON-LEAGUE ROUTE

It's the 2015/2016 Premier League campaign and Leicester City sit at the top of the league. It is history happening before my eyes, as I write this book. Jamie Vardy, Leicester City's striker, has been sensational this season and has scored twenty-two goals. Jamie also broke the record by becoming the first player to score in eleven consecutive Premier League matches. Now, for everybody reading this book that doesn't know who Jamie Vardy is...

He is an inspiration to many young players around the country that dreams can come true. Jamie Vardy was released from Sheffield Wednesday Academy at age sixteen, apparently for being too small. He became disillusioned with football and stopped playing. Jamie admits it was a low point and a real heartache to get over. Eventually, Jamie was convinced by a friend to start playing football again. He made his way up from the lower tiers of English football and played for Stockbridge Park Steels, Halifax Town, and Fleetwood Town. Leicester City then paid Fleetwood Town one million pounds for Jamie Vardy, and here we are today with Leicester City top of the Premier League and Jamie Vardy joint top scorer. What makes Jamie's journey even more spectacular is that we are in a time when kids and teenagers would rather spend more time inside playing Xbox and PlayStation than going outside to kick a ball about. Hopefully, Jamie has shown aspiring football players that hard work and belief in yourself might get you to the top or to have a career in football.

Jamie is not the only player to make his way up the leagues. Chris Smalling was at non-league Maidstone, went to Fulham, and then was signed by Manchester United. Charlie Austin was another player released from Reading Academy for supposedly being too small. Charlie Austin went from non-league football to League One with Swindon Town. He then moved to Burnley in the Championship and from Burnley to Queens Park Rangers, who were in the Premier League at the time. He finished the season with eighteen goals and was the fourth top scorer in the Premier League. He has now moved to Southampton, and I believe he will establish himself as a top English Premier League striker. Dwight Gayle, another player released by Arsenal Academy, worked his way up from non-league to play for Crystal Palace. The academy system let down three players. A system that the England national team is relying on for talented players to be produced, a system the football clubs themselves don't put complete faith into. If the clubs did, less money would be spent on foreign players, and less foreign youth players would be drafted into the academy setup. I always wonder why the lower pro clubs loan in youth players from the big pro clubs and all these clubs have their own youth setup. Wouldn't you give your own youth an opportunity instead of another club's youth? These are the types of actions that show there is no faith in the academy setup, so why should I have faith in the system?

Down in the lower tier of English football, many talented players are hungry for an opportunity. I have named four players that have come from the lower leagues, and I could keep listing talented people that have come from the lower leagues and are now playing at the highest level. There is definitely talent down in the lower leagues. What's going? Why are we not seeing more talent being picked up by top Premier League clubs? When was the last time a top Premier League club bought a player from a non-league club?

Non-league players would find it more difficult to adapt to an academy environment because of the competitive nature down in non-league. More players play on the edge in non-league football, and these players can be seen as difficult to work with. I am a strong believer that there is a thin line between nightmare and genius. Players from non-league football can have too much of a personality, and these types of players would not last long in academies. Coaches in academies won't work with players with too much personality; they want players to do what they want and do what they say. When players are different and have an edge to them, they can be looked upon as problematic. Having an edge should be a good thing, whether that is their personality or their training. There has to be a reason that makes someone great, and if you take that away, they are not the same player or person. Non-league players can sometimes have a chequered past; these types of players can be off-putting to pro clubs. Some of the greatest boxers in history have a chequered past. Lots of boxers have spoken about boxing saving them and keeping them focused and on the straight and narrow. Are talented people expected to have a squeaky-clean background? I know my background is not perfect.

I grew up in Peckham and, according to statistics, it is currently the worst place to live in London. There is a lot of poverty and struggling single parents, which creates the perfect breeding ground for crime and violence. Growing up, there were a lot of talented people there, but now many of them are dead, in jail, or addicted to drugs. Peckham has produced Rio Ferdinand and Anton Ferdinand, who have gone on to play for professional football clubs. I grew up with Marlon King and used to play football with him and his older brother Dean. We would play football on the estate. Marlon's dad, Carl, who I thought was an amazing dad, decided that Marlon was getting into too much trouble, so Marlon left Peckham and lived with his dad and went on to become a professional footballer. I was jealous of Marlon's relationship with his dad. My dad was not around much; I only saw him when I was in trouble, but I was not unique. It was the same story for most single parents living in Peckham. Nathaniel Thomson, better known as Giggs, a rapper from Peckham. John Boyega, who stars in *Star Wars: The Force Awakens.* Peckham is not doing too badly.

Non-league football is important to aspiring footballers trying to achieve a career in something they love. You don't get judged for your past, just for your performance. This football gives hope to players that are told they are too small, not quick enough, and too old. Non-league football could easily become the source for the next generation of stars. Maybe the perception of non-league football is that it is a bunch of overweight players, who are straight in the pub after the match. The attitude of players in non-league clubs is totally different. Players are seeing what is possible. If you believe and take it seriously, players from the lower tier of English football are looking after themselves.

In non-league football, players need to stay motivated through injuries and setbacks, which helps to develop a strong stickability and persistence. I do believe that with more players seeing non-league football as a route to carve out a career as a footballer, we will get more players climbing to the top of English football.

Non-league players are playing football because they love football first. Players don't get into non-league football for the money; the money is low, which is why the majority of players have jobs. This type of football is also important to players trying to rebuild their career. It's a safety net for players who need a level to fall back on and rise from. The standard at non-league will probably surprise a lot of people. Non-league is filled with academy releases and players trying to rebuild their career. If there is one thing I can say about non-league football, it is that it offers hope to all the thousands of young footballers tossed aside by the pro academies. I believe non-league football is vitally important to English grassroots football. It's football that provides a route for the players that are not lucky enough to be picked up by a pro academy. More players will look at non-league football as a route to having a career in football. Maybe in the past it seemed like an impossible route, but more young players are realising that it's more important to play football at the highest level possible and perform. Professional football players like Jamie Vardy have shown that anything is possible.

In the past few years, the perception has been that pro academies are the only way to have a career in football, even though lots of football players started in non-league football. We don't hear as much about them as we do the academy players. Perhaps because most players that come through non-league are academy rejects. It does not put academies in a good light. A lot of the problems in English football have been blamed on pro academies. Academies do have their problems, but non-league football has not been seen as a place for talented players; clubs and scouts don't want to take the risk, why? English clubs are more than willing to take the risk on players from abroad, but not on players in the same country, players that are used to the physicality of English football. Is it that much of a risk? Maybe pro clubs feel English players are not good enough. Leicester City took the risk of buying Jamie Vardy for one million; is one million a risk? Would that be a risk to the top teams in England? Top Premier League teams have paid that in agent fees. How much is Jamie Vardy worth to Leicester City now? Thirty million, forty million? English talent is highly inflated. Quality English players are considered rare, which makes them expensive, and it does not have to be that way. Non-league should be the first place to look for talent instead of going abroad. The potential to find untapped English talent down in non-league football should be attractive. I am impressed with what Eddie Howe is doing at Bournemouth FC. Most teams that get promoted to the Premier League go after experienced players, sometimes players that are past their best, but Eddie has gone after young English players. I would love Canaan to play for him, a fantastic young manager with a different mindset.

In football, there is a herd mentality. When a big Premier club is interested in a player, all of a sudden a whole bunch of clubs are interested in that player. We see it now: when a player is released from a club or academy, another club is more likely to give that player an opportunity rather than give an opportunity to a player that is unknown. If more Premier League Clubs were down in the non-league looking to unearth talent like Jamie Vardy and more and more talent were proving themselves at the top level, it would become a real viable source to find talented players. The reality is that football clubs want players in their respective league, players that are playing at the same level or a higher level. Pro teams are more than happy to buy foreign players from abroad and take the risk on foreign talent, rather than take the risk on talent closer to home; maybe because English talent is too expensive? Is it down to the scouting? The top Premier League clubs have a vast scouting network across Europe, but how much scouting is done in England?

Canaan has played the majority of his football in the Highbury and Islington area, and I can honestly say that in eight years at grassroots, I have never seen or met an Arsenal scout. Not only that, but Canaan was captain of his primary school and his primary school is the closest to the Emirates Stadium. His secondary school is the closest to the Emirates Stadium. He represented Islington District and was playing for the best junior club in Islington. What else could he have done to get noticed by the team that he loves and supports? It was only when he went to an Arsenal Kicks session in Hackney that he was invited down to the Arsenal Development Centre. Unfortunately, the opportunity came at the wrong time for Canaan because of injuries and fitness. The scouts I have met in the Islington area are from Brentford FC and Southampton FC. Brentford were the most active in pursuing players from Canaan's junior club, Isledon Wolves. Brentford wanted to do a deal with Isledon Wolves on first choice of players but pulled out when Isledon Wolves were working with other clubs. Oh yeah, I met Norwich scouts too, but never an Arsenal scout. Can you be scouted by your local professional team anymore?

Non-league players are relying on scouts from the Championship, League One and League Two clubs. League One and League Two, I believe, will have the most scouts down in non-league, and these are the clubs that don't have the biggest resources and I imagine not the biggest network of scouts. It then comes down to the scouts being brave enough to recommend non-league players that they believe can make the grade. Obviously, scouts don't want to get it wrong because it's their job on the line. With Jamie Vardy putting a massive spotlight on non-league football, hopefully, we will see more scouts down in non-league and more clubs willing to take a risk on non-league football. If more players are being bought from non-league, it will have a ripple effect through grassroots football. It will be extra motivation for young players to work hard and become totally dedicated. There is a big difference to being in an academy, hoping and praying for an opportunity in the first team, compared to being bought by a club and that club making an investment in a player. It will also mean that age will mean nothing, and talented football players will keep believing as they get older. I totally believe that if more Premier clubs were buying non-league players, it would totally transform non-league football. It would also help to generate more income for non-league clubs as every bit of money helps to keep the non-league clubs thriving.

Canaan is determined to follow down the non-league route and has more than enough belief in his ability. He knows that if you put him on a football field and tell him to go and produce, he will. Coaches have reinforced his belief too. His mission is to keep trying to play at the highest level possible. Canaan knows he is not the quickest or most dynamic, but he knows his strengths and keeps trying to improve those strengths as well as his weaknesses, but the focus is always his strengths, which is where his talent is. He is going into a part of his development where he is playing semi-pro football. Coaches like Canaan; he has an excellent attitude and has always left an impact on the teams he has played for. The theme has never changed; coaches believe Canaan is talented. It helps to keep Canaan believing and growing his confidence to chase his dream of becoming a footballer. Ideally, every boy's dream is to play for the team he has supported his whole life, but ultimately, Canaan wants to have a career in something he loves doing, and that is playing football. Right now, he has a few choices of semi-pro teams to play for. One of the teams he was interested in was too far. Distance and travel time has to make sense to be able to commit and remain focused.

Do pro football academies work? The jury is still out on that one. It depends on what we mean by work. There are definitely some positives to football academies: consistent training and coaching at least three times a week. Generally, some football academies have an ethos or philosophy that they abide by when developing young football players. The facilities are some of the best in the world, state of the art. Top pro clubs have spent millions on their academies, even hiring nutritionists, physios, and psychologists to offer advice on mental preparation, and diet. Some of the best English world-class talents have come through the academy system. If you have spent most of your life training at a football academy, week in week out, not having the same worries that you get at a junior club like the standard of coaching, there is no comparison on between the level of your development and that of players being coached by a local junior club. Currently, the academy system seems to be only producing good players; they are not producing exceptional players. In the past, academies have produced world-class players like Paul Scholes, Steven Gerrard, David Beckham, Frank Lampard, and Wayne Rooney. These football players can win matches on their own. Players that can produce a bit of magic and change the outcome of the match. English football academies are not producing players of that quality on a consistent basis, and maybe it might have something to do with how many opportunities academy players are getting in the first team. With 65 percent of academy players released each year, maybe there is some world-class talent, but we never see it.

The academy environment is set up for young players to conform or be released. A player coming into the academy setup who is a free spirit and has played most of his football in the streets or local junior club is used to expressing himself and trying different things on a football pitch. He comes with a rawness and creative spark about him. When this type of player enters the academy setup, problems start to arise. The ironic thing is that the creative spark and inventiveness that helped get him spotted by a scout will be the first attributes of the player's game to be coached out. Remember the academies' mantra is 'keep it simple'. 'Keep it simple' creates good players, not world-class players. World-class players are not simple, they are amazing. Young players entering the academy setup should be developed to become strong individuals, and the talent they have should be nurtured and built upon, but the mindset seems to be that anything you did prior to entering the academy is wrong. There is no faith in junior club football development. Junior clubs are a place to find young players. Academies like to get players in as kids so they don't pick up bad habits-according to the academies. What are bad habits? Habits like expressing yourself and being creative and inventive. Are these bad habits?

Academies want to develop strong teams with team play and tactical systems. Should young kids be worrying about team play and tactical systems? There will come a time in a young kid's development where it will be time to learn about tactical systems and team play. When kids are young, the most important thing should be that they are enjoying their football and can express themselves on a football pitch. Young kids should be given the confidence to try new skills and to beat other players. Development should be focused on each individual, improving both feet, close control, and touch. But in academies, the focus seems to be on team functionality.

Parents are becoming wiser to the football academies and are not happy to go along with what the academy wants without asking questions. Parents who I have spoken to are questioning whether academy football is the best thing for their kid. Academy recruiters will dangle lucrative contracts and fantastic opportunities to the players, putting on pressure and timescales to accept their contracts. Academies are in the perfect position to abuse their power, playing on millions of young aspiring footballers' dreams: 'If you don't sign with us, how else are you going to become a footballer?' Fortunately, more parents are doing their homework and want to know the track record of the academy giving young players an opportunity. Some of the big clubs in England have a diabolical track record in giving English talent an opportunity, and parents need to know this.

When it comes to the pro academies, one of the biggest problems is that no one knows what goes on in an academy environment until they are a part of the setup. Academies answer to no one; you don't know if they have your kid's best interests at heart. Something else which is not foreseen by parents is the long-term effects that being in an academy environment can have on kids. Schoolwork can become affected, and if kids do not stay grounded, they can start developing an ego. It's easy for them to believe that they are going to be a footballer and not put in the same effort in school. Being in an academy from nine years old, they can start to not appreciate the opportunity and become ungrateful.

These are some of the regrets that parents have had, and other parents should know. We know it's down to the parents to keep their kids on the straight and narrow, but it can be difficult, especially for single parents. When kids have been in an academy environment from a young age, we can get ten and eleven-year-olds believing they are going to be rich, and this can change their mindset when it about school.

Let's say your eleven-year-old has been offered a place at the academy and signs his schoolboy forms. When that happens, I believe three massive changes have occurred in your kid's life. I am highlighting these changes because academies don't make parents clear on the commitment that will be expected from them. Parents are expected to figure it out. How do you tell your eleven-year-old that it is not possible to commit when they are excited at the possibility of joining a pro academy and fulfilling their dream? Parents then go head first into doing whatever the academy wants, and the academies know this. The first change will be travelling to and from the academy. Academies train two or three times a week and have a match on Sunday, and some of these academies are in the middle of nowhere. Therefore, due to the location of some of these academies, it would be impossible not to have a car. If you don't have a car, I don't know how you will get there.

An academy was interested in a teenager I know who is a talented defender, but his mum had no interest in her son's football and his dad was not around. There was a problem with him travelling to the academy as he was still quite young, and the academy was a bit of a distance from his house. The academy decided to sign the teenager in question and his best friend. The friend's mum used to take them both to training. Once the teenager I know was able to make his own way to the academy, the academy released his friend. How ruthless is that? It's the inside stories from parents that no one hears about. Two training sessions could be held on school nights and don't forget the match on Sunday. Sometimes Canaan would have a match after school and if he had an early kickoff, he just about had enough time to change into his football kit even though he was around the corner from the football pitch. Travelling long distances can be stressful and exhausting, not to mention stressful for the parent driving through rush hour or at dangerous speeds because you want to get there on time. Remember the school holidays and all the football tournaments that you will have to travel to; be prepared to drop family events because sacrifices will have to be made.

Maybe you're reading this and thinking, *I will get help from the football club with the travel and expense.* It's possible you might get some help from the club, but the way I look at it is that if a football club wants to sign a young player they have a strong interest in, they are going to move heaven and earth to sign that player. It has been no secret of the lengths football clubs will go to secure a young player's signature. They might offer private school education or even buy a house for the parents. If the club is not offering incentives to get your kid to sign, then you probably won't get the help for travel. This information is not to put academies in a bad light; I want parents to know what they are getting into before their kid signs. It can at least help parents to negotiate better, and we have to remember that the club has the club's best interest at heart and the parent must have their kid's best interest at heart.

The second change for your kid will be that football isn't fun anymore. Once a young player signs the contract, he is now playing football to get the contract renewed and keep his place in the academy. The performances must be of a high level consistently, and you can't get ill or injured because you don't want to give the coach an excuse to drop you from the team. Parents have told me that they are scared to tell the coach when their kid is not feeling well. The pressure on the kids and parents can be incredible. We have to remember that this can be kids as young as nine.

When Canaan started playing football, it was important to me that football stayed fun for as long as possible. I knew he loved it and I wanted him to keep that love. Which is why I waited before introducing him to competitive football. Once kids enter a pro academy, they are exposed to a ruthless, stressful environment and are quickly released when progressing slowly. The attitude from academies is, throw enough shit on the wall and hopefully some will stick. How much pressure is on your kid when everything he does is carefully analysed and monitored?

My third and final point is now that your kid is signed up and a part of the academy setup, in a sense, your kid now belongs to them. I have heard that some academies encourage the young players to play other sports, but not all academies. Some academies put restrictions on what sports and activities the players can do. A simple game of playing football over at the park is out of the question. I know some kids that have been too scared to do other sports in school because they fear getting injured. The threat of getting released is always there, and if you get an injury, it does not feel like too long before you're out the door.

All I want to do with this book is give parents a better understanding and clarity on things that the academies do not make you aware of. Let's say everything is going well; as a parent, you have managed to fit everything around work and are able to keep up with the demands of the academy. A schoolboy contract is usually renewed every year or two years. Once he turns sixteen years old, if he is one of the lucky ones, he will be offered a scholarship on the youth training scheme. Research found that 98 percent of kids that join academies will be released by eighteen years old and less than 1 percent go on to become professional footballers. Does that sound like a system that is working? Once a scholarship is offered, it can last three years, and when the three years is up, the club will decide whether or not they offer you a pro contract. Years of training with an academy and you will only know if you have a future at the club when you turn nineteen years old. A high-risk long-term investment. To me, it makes more sense to go out there and play as much football as possible at different levels, gain all the experience you can from different teams and leagues, work with lots of different coaches, focus on fine-tuning your game with competitive football, and build interest and relationships in football.

According to the Premier League and Football League, between 60 percent and 65 percent of seven hundred scholars taken on each year are rejected at eighteen years old. The Professional Footballers' Association reckons that half of those scholars that win a full-time contract will not be playing at a professional level by twenty-one. Of under nines, 0.5 percent are likely to make it to the first team. When we look at the stats, you can see how shocking the numbers are. If this was a school you were considering for your kid, it wouldn't even make it as an option. How many parents know how successful the pro academies are? All that pressure and stress and less than 1 percent actually make it out of the academies into professional football. There seems to be this misconception that unless you are in an academy, there is no possible way to have a career in football. Before football academies, you had to play for your school, district team, and county team. Because of the lack of support, district football seems to be disappearing. When Canaan did district football, Mike and Warren were volunteering their time and effort for the district team and relying on donations. If you did manage to get spotted playing for your district team by a pro club, you could be offered a two-year apprenticeship, which was a YTS scheme, known as a youth training scheme. The scheme would start when you turned sixteen years old, the pay was about £30 a week and you would be expected to do odd jobs around the clubs. There was no need to take kids in from nine years old.

Let's say, against all the odds, your kid is one of the lucky ones and he gets offered a pro contract; at this point, he will be a young man. The sacrifices and years of training have finally paid off. He gets that pro contract and the future is looking bright. It has been known that some youth players can earn up to twenty thousand a week, and this can bring a lot of its own problems. The biggest problem of all is getting an opportunity in the first team. With the pro clubs having millions of pounds at their disposal, they can go and buy any player and youth player from around the world. What happens when the club decides to go and buy a youth player for ten million pounds, the same age as your son; who gets priority in the first team? Who will be more likely to get the first opportunities in the first team?

Pro clubs buy and sell players every year, and academy players get fewer opportunities to break through into the first team. How much faith do the clubs have in their own academies? I can't answer that question, especially as some clubs loan out other clubs' academy players instead of giving opportunities to their own academy players. What I hear over and over is that managers are under so much pressure for results that they don't want to take the chance on youth. What's the point then? All it shows is that the clubs have no faith in their own academy system, and if they don't have faith in it, why should I have faith in the system for my son?

Maybe because they are a big respected pro club and I should accept that they know what they are doing and are the professionals. A slight problem with that: when it comes to bringing through home-grown youth players, the big pro clubs' record is the worst. Research group CIES Football Observatory have found that the Premier League is the worst league in Europe for home-grown players to get an opportunity and some of the top teams are the worst offenders. These are the realities for parents when their kid has been scouted for an academy, and I don't believe that it is clear for parents to see before a contract has been signed. Canaan and I have stayed away from academies and not pursued those types of opportunities. Through his short football journey, he has enjoyed playing for different junior clubs and getting lots of different experiences in his development. Canaan has had some ups and downs but nothing as devastating and traumatising as being released from an academy. Some kids that have been released fall totally out of love with football, and with the stats not supporting the academy system, why would I want to put Canaan through that pressure with the threat of always being released? It doesn't look like it will get any better for home-grown talent. A study by CIES Football Observatory found that 66 percent of players in the Premier League were foreign. Home-grown players in the Premier League decreased from 72 percent in 1992 to the current 31 percent. Russia seems to be experiencing the same problem with a rich, domestic league dominated by the wealthiest clubs, which are struggling to unearth home-grown talent.

END OF AN ERA

After the initial shock of Isledon Wolves folding, Canaan and I came to the realisation that we would have to find a new junior club. Canaan didn't want to because Adrian was his coach, and Adrian understood him. He had got to know him well over the last three years. The last three years had been fantastic for his development and now it was all coming to an end. The motivation to go and play for another local junior club was not there. Who was he going to play for? He had been playing for the best team in Islington. At the time, I never had any idea of a team Canaan could play for, and there was no need to take other coaches' numbers as Canaan was completely happy at Isledon Wolves and with Adrian. All these years later, after I set out with Canaan to develop him into a technical football player, we were at a crossroads. Canaan was not even sure he wanted to play for another grassroots junior club. What could they offer him? He had won everything; he had been working with the best grassroots coach in Islington, in his opinion. It was a confusing time, and we were not sure what direction to go in. I then got a phone call from Adrian, and he was recommending Regents Park FC. Adrian told me that the guy who ran Regents Park was asking for players, and he gave me the guy's number. Adrian told me to check it out because he was not sure what they were like. As I have said before, Isledon Wolves were the best team at that time and we had beaten many teams, including Regents Park. I even remember when Isledon Wolves demolished Regents Park 10-1. Isledon Wolves always beat them comprehensively. I never could imagine Canaan would play for them. I didn't even want to tell Canaan that Regents Park was looking for players. After I finished speaking to Adrian, I went to Canaan's room, knocked on his door, and went in. Canaan was playing *Fifa* on his PlayStation. When I told him Regents Park were looking for new players.

Canaan agreed to check them out, but he wanted to keep his options open. He wasn't enthusiastic but, at the same time, he didn't want to start the new season without a new football team. I rang the number that Adrian gave me, and the guy I spoke to was called John. He explained to me that the under fifteens for the new season would be training at Regents Park on Saturdays. John also told me the coach's name was Kevin. I thanked John and got off the phone. The following Saturday, I drove Canaan to Regents Park. It was not a new venue to us as we had played for Pro Touch Academy at Regents Park. Canaan was still unsure and didn't think the standard in the Regents Park League was high. In his mind, it felt like going backwards, but he was trying to stay positive.

When we got to Regents Park, there were football teams everywhere. It was difficult to find a group of boys that looked Canaan's age. I asked someone wearing a Regents Park FC shirt to point me in the right direction to Kevin, and he did. I found Kevin and the group of boys. I explained who we were and we introduced ourselves. Kevin knew Canaan was coming from Isledon Wolves; he was coming with a reputation. Canaan grabbed a ball and joined in the training session.

While the lads were training, Kevin and I had a chat and he explained to me that the current training session was the last one because, every year, the team flew out to Sweden to compete in the Gothia Cup. The Gothia Cup was the biggest youth cup competition in Europe and was open to anyone. I wish they did more big cups like this at grassroots level; it could definitely help to give more players opportunities to play at the highest level around Europe. Kevin told me that for the new season, Regents Park would be entering the Harrow League and it would be the first year the boys would be competing in the Harrow League. Kevin's attention turned to Canaan, who was doing what he does best when he has a football at his feet. Kevin was saying how Canaan was strong, had quick feet, and did not stop working. Some of the Regents Park players knew Canaan was from Isledon Wolves, and it meant Canaan came with expectations. It didn't take long for Kevin to want to sign him up. I was still unsure of how Canaan felt about the team, but he was enjoying himself in training.

After the training session, Kevin told me to go to the hub and talk to someone about fees and signing up. The hub was in the middle of Regents Park; it had a canteen and changing rooms. The hub was busy with lots of coaches and players all over the place. The person I had to talk to was a lady I knew. I had met her when Canaan was playing for the district team. Her son had also been selected for the district team and was a good player. He was a battler and was absolutely fearless; that was when he was eleven years old. This was a nice surprise and after having a good chat with her and catching up, she told me Regents Park was a well-run club and organised. As she was telling me about fees and the club's code of conduct, Kevin interrupted and said we needed to sign up.

Kevin spoke with the lady a little bit, then turned to leave. I wished him luck in the Gothia Cup and told him that I would see him when he got back. I spoke to the lady I knew for a little bit longer and filled out some forms, and she gave me some leaflets with information about the club. After that, Canaan and I left.

On the drive home, I was interested to know what Canaan thought. He had definitely warmed up to the idea of playing for Regents Park, but what was bothering him was playing in the Regents Park League; he felt the standard was poor. He didn't want to drop out from playing in the Harrow League to the Regents Park League and didn't want to play in the Camden and Islington League. It felt good to be able to tell him that Regents Park would be competing in the Harrow League next season. That was all Canaan needed to hear. Playing in the Harrow League and the opportunity to go to the Gothia Cup next year was enough to seal the deal.

Canaan was telling me the group of players were welcoming to him and told him they had lost some attacking players, but thought he was better than them.

What I didn't know is that I wouldn't have to wait until Kevin got back. I got a call from the club owner, John, a few days later. John wanted to get Canaan signed up as soon as possible. *Kevin must have spoken to him,* I thought. John told me he needed four photos and for Canaan to sign two registration forms. John gave me his address in Highgate. I met a lady at the address as John was not there. Canaan signed the forms, dropped off the photos, and left. I got a call from Kevin when he got back. He was going to start training at Hampstead Heath. Kevin told me his players had done well in the Gothia Cup but eventually got knocked out by the team that won the tournament. Canaan was looking forward to starting training with his new teammates.

After years of Canaan playing football, it's easy for us to get a feel for a new coach quite quickly.

Kevin was a likeable guy and passionate about his football. I guess the problem for Kevin was Canaan had worked with coaches who we thought were top class. He had been at Isledon Wolves for three years working with Adrian, and in that time, Canaan's game had improved. Adrian liked movement and interchanging, Adrian's teams did not have fixed positions, and it's what Canaan had been working on for the last three years; it was a part of his game. I hoped Kevin would get to know Canaan and understand his game as I could foresee problems if he didn't. Regents Park was a well-run club. It was the first junior club where I could pay my fees online. They had their own merchandise, training tops, scarves, and hats. I had to go to the shop to buy Canaan's kit. This was much different to other junior clubs, where cash was handed over in brown envelopes and I would pick the kit out of the boot of a car. Also, Kevin would email diagrams of the upcoming training session with the drills he would be doing. I thought this was an excellent idea, and I had never seen a coach do that before. Another brilliant website Kevin would use was Teamer.net. This website was an amazing team management website with the option to download the app. With Teamer, Kevin was able to know whether you were available for the match with a week's notice, and he would pick the team on Teamer. At training, no one knew if they had been selected for the match. If you didn't turn up for training, then you couldn't be surprised if you were not selected for the match. I love that: training focused on training. All the details of the match were on Teamer, and you had to train and perform, no one was given special treatment, and everybody was on equal footing. Canaan loved that. Teamer meant the players were not under pressure to be at the match. In the past, Canaan would get down on himself if he couldn't make it to the match because of unforeseen circumstances and felt he was letting the team down, especially at Isledon Wolves because the numbers were low. Teamer allowed Kevin to know who was available and who wasn't long before match day. He could then offer the place on the team to someone else who never made the squad. Teamer is a fantastic idea that I highly recommend to any football coach.

In the size difference between Isledon Wolves FC and Regents Park FC, there is no comparison. Regents Park has over twenty-three coaches, all of different age groups with sometimes two or three teams in the same age group. It's a massive junior club. Isledon Wolves had been more successful in the last three years.

I was in Canaan's room chilling, watching a football match with him, when he got a notification on his phone from Teamer. There was an upcoming match at Market Road against St John's Wood. At the end of the last season, Canaan had no interest in playing at Market Road in the Camden and Islington League, but during the close season, Aquaterra, who was responsible for the majority of leisure centres in Islington, including Market Road, lost the contract to GLL. GLL stands for Greenwich Leisure Limited, which is a non profit organisation that runs sport and leisure facilities on behalf of the local authorities. The contract meant an investment of ten million would be spent on the facilities over the next fifteen years.

The changes were rapid; the tired old pitch at Market Road, which had been there since my girlfriend was a little girl, had been torn out and brand-new 3G Astro pitches had been laid in their place. The pitches had been caged off. Only coaches and the teams were allowed on the pitch. The parents could shout support and make noise, but it was from a distance. This was a lot better for the young kids that would sometimes become overwhelmed by parents screaming at them. All the kids had to worry about was the coach's voice. Canaan was itching to play on the new pitches and decided he would play one more season in the Camden and Islington League to get to play on those new pitches at Market Road. After that, he wanted to focus on playing eleven-a-side football on grass. Canaan accepted on Teamer and was looking forward to match day.

St John's Wood was who Regents Park was playing in their first match in the Camden and Islington League match. The current champions and cup champions, this was the team that had taken over from Isledon Wolves. Match day felt extra busy. Kevin told me how he knew the St John's Wood coach well and they would have lots of banter on who was going to beat whom. Match day was lively, and it felt like most of Islington was out to see the new pitches. While I was looking around admiring the changes at Market Road, I got a tap on the shoulder. It was Kevin pointing at a man in front of me; he told me he was a scout from Brentford FC. He was here to look at a player from St John's Wood. The player he was looking at had been signed by Queens Park Rangers FC, but the player had left because of the travelling distance. He was tall, big, and strong. He looked more like a man and didn't look like he belonged in the under fifteens. Apparently, he was American. In my mind, the stage was set. Canaan versus the American player. The match started at a fast and furious pace. There were chances for both teams in the first five minutes.

The American player was big, strong, quick, and dynamic, exactly the type of player the scouts love in England. It made sense with the interest in him. The ball broke free and the American player was onto it in a flash. He picked up the ball and drove straight down the middle towards Regents Park's defence. He then slowed down, looked up, and hit a beautiful shot towards the top corner of the goal. No chance for the goalkeeper, the ball flew right into the top corner. St John's Wood's teammates were celebrating and hugging. Kevin was shouting from the sidelines.

'Don't worry, lads, pick your heads up and let's go.'

The ball went back to the centre and Regents Park got the game underway again. Canaan was playing on the wing, but he had the freedom to drift infield. Canaan picked up the ball deep in his own half. He then dribbled with the ball until an opposing player started to close him. He then passed the ball out to the wing where another of his players had taken up position. The player did a little turn and beat an opponent and was off running down the wing.

Canaan started running too, killing himself to keep up with the play. A low cross into the box and Canaan arrived into the box right on cue, a side foot finish right into the bottom corner. There were screams and celebrations, game on 1-1. St John's Wood got the game underway. Regents Park was the team everybody expected to beat, but St John's Wood knew they were in for a game today. The American player was absolutely causing havoc every time he was on the ball. He was an absolute menace. Then you had Canaan, who was in a confident mood after scoring his goal. When confidence is flowing through Canaan, he is such a threat. He was terrorising with his constant dribbling and quick feet. The American player received the ball and he was quickly closed down, but because he was strong, he managed to keep a hold of the ball and broke free, bearing down on Regents Park's defence. He then hit a ferocious shot, which slammed against the post. The power in the shot shook the whole goal. The ball was bobbling about and the goalkeeper and Regents Park players were scrambling around to get the ball away, but one of the St John's Wood's players poked the ball into the goal. This was a devastating blow to Regents Park to give a goal away after getting the equaliser. The Regents Park players looked deflated, like they were ready to give up. Canaan wasn't; he was talking to his teammates trying to encourage them. For him St John's Wood was a team he beat plenty of times with Isledon Wolves and, in his heart, he still felt they were beatable.

The match kicked off again, the score was 2-1 to St John's Wood. Canaan was working his socks off and pressing the St John's Wood defenders. Hard work and pressing had become a part of his game because of working with Adrian. The hard work Canaan was putting in was about to pay off. As Canaan was pressing the defenders, one of the defenders got caught in two minds and ended up dwelling on the ball, the opportunity Canaan was looking for. He went in hard with a strong tackle on the defender and won the ball. The defender then tried to recover but slipped, and Canaan was off. Another defender tried to come across and cover, but Canaan put the ball through his legs and dribbled towards the goal. He was now one-on-one with the goalkeeper, and I love Canaan in one-on-one situations. I think Canaan loves it too. Cool, calm, and collected, he slotted the ball into the bottom corner.

Two-two and Kevin was celebrating on the touchline, fist pumping the air. Canaan was celebrating with his teammates. The scout was still watching the match, and I had been watching him when Canaan scored the goal. His reactions seemed to be of excitement, but he could have been enjoying the match. It had been an entertaining match. The game kicked off again and the referee quickly blew for halftime. I was proud of Canaan. He was getting off to a good start with his new club. It was beautiful to see his development over the years and all the different aspects to his game which he had worked on since he was a kid. We were getting to see the benefits now he is fifteen years old. I saw Canaan getting his reward from his work rate, and I remembered how his work rate was before we met Adrian. There was such a massive difference, and now that work rate was a part of his game. The goals and assists he has got over the years from working hard have made him believe in the importance of working hard. Watching his runs and movement, all attributes that have been added to his game, I was the proudest dad. I know how hard Canaan works to get better and keep getting better. When someone has that type of attitude to their development, with that type of dedication and commitment, then it doesn't matter what their body shape is or how fast they can run. You can have the most talented player with blistering pace and a beautiful athletic body shape, but if they have a poor attitude and lack commitment and dedication, it won't matter how good they are.

The second half kicked off and St John's Wood was fired up. They started strong, putting Regents Park under immediate pressure. Regents Park was just about holding on from conceding another goal, with the goalkeeper making a string of saves. St John's Wood kept piling on the pressure, with the American player involved in everything. Eventually, the pressure was too much, and St John's Wood scored the goal. They quickly doubled their lead. Canaan managed to hit the post and had a few shots saved by the goalkeeper. Regents Park had a few more chances, but the game ended 4-2 to St John's Wood. A great effort from Regents Park, but St John's Wood was too strong. Canaan was happy with his impact in his first Camden and Islington League game for Regents Park but was not happy with the final result.

 After the match ended, the scout who had been watching the game quickly made his way over to the St John's Wood coach. I knew Canaan had an excellent performance today; he scored two goals and his overall game had been excellent. It's always nice to perform in front of scouts, but he has on many different occasions. It's rare for a scout to turn up at a match to see what players are good. In my experience, scouts are usually at a match to see someone and most of the time they never stay for the whole match. If you haven't got blistering pace, they lose interest. If you're not big and strong, they lose interest. If you don't have a certain body shape and are not dynamic, they lose interest. The focus for Canaan is and has always been to master his craft, to keep improving day by day, to try and get a little bit better every day. Master the timing of his runs, work on his movement, and find space on the pitch to keep improving his game intelligence and building consistency. Put him in an eleven-a-side football team and tell him to perform and he will get goals, assists, and work his socks off; it's what he does and will continue to do.

'Another Teamer has come through.

Dad, I have accepted.'

Canaan's next match was in the Harrow League; Regents Park was playing LNR. Driving to Harrow for Canaan's away games had become the norm now. We had been doing this for the last two years with Isledon Wolves. The difference this time was that Canaan was the only one to have experienced playing in the Harrow League. This was a new experience for the Regents Park team. Kevin had told Canaan that he would give him an opportunity in his favoured role of attacking midfield. That's all Canaan wanted: the opportunity to cement his spot on the team as an attacking midfielder and perform in that role. It's hard to have any excuses when you are given a chance in the position you want. It's up to the player to then perform. Canaan was also given the number 10 shirt, his favourite shirt number, and he was so pumped he could not wait for kickoff. The grass pitch was at a decent standard. Some of these pitches can be shocking, especially when it rains. The match got underway and Canaan had an extra energy about him. He was bubbly and in the mood. *The other team is in trouble,* I thought. With Canaan's first touch of the ball, he dribbled at the opposition and delivered a beautiful through ball with the outside of his boot, right into the path of the striker, who then went around the goalkeeper to put Regents Park in the lead. Canaan was on fire; everything he was doing was coming off. Two more delicious through balls for both the wingers and both took their chances; Regents Park then scored another goal and it was four, nil by halftime. Canaan had been involved in three of the goals.

Second half started and LNR decided to man-mark Canaan. I can't blame them. He was a constant threat whenever he got the ball. That meant a dedicated player would stay with Canaan at all times. I don't like it when coaches tell a player to stick to an opposing player for the whole match. How does that help the player's development? If results and winning are what is important to the coach, then he won't care about sacrificing one of his player's development to track a player all over the pitch. Coaches forget the main focus should be youth development. Where is the development in making a player chase another player all over the pitch? The player that was given the task to stick to Canaan, quite frankly, didn't want to do it. He never caused problems for Canaan, but I thought it would have been good for Canaan's development to deal with a man-marker.

The game finished 7-2 and Canaan was the creator of four of the goals. He should have scored as well. He hit the post and the crossbar. Regents Park had got off to an excellent start, but it was all for nothing as the ID cards had not been processed in time, which meant the points went to LNR and Regents Park had got off to a losing start. During the week, Canaan and I were in shock when we checked the league table to see Regents Park was bottom of the league. Kevin fumed about losing the points but vowed that would be the only points taken off Regents Park this season.

The next few games were in the Camden and Islington League at Market Road, and Regents Park was not doing as well in the Camden and Islington League as they were doing in the Harrow League. They had only played one game in the Harrow League, but you could tell Regents Park was definitely more suited to eleven-a-side football. I have mentioned before in this book that there is a big difference between playing on Astro and grass. Playing on Astro can be end to end; the ball rolls quicker and it's seven a-side with no offside. Some of the Regents Park players struggled to keep up with the intensity that seven a-side football is played at. A lot of the Regents Park players were more comfortable playing on grass. Someone watching Regents Park play on Astro may think these players were no good, but on grass, these players excelled and Regents Park was a different team. I know Canaan is ten times better on grass than he is on Astro. He does not enjoy football on Astro as much as he does on grass. It's one of the reasons I believe more Astro pitches won't solve the problems at grassroots. In the media, it seems to be the reason why grassroots football is struggling. More Astro pitches will help with training; it depends if junior clubs can afford the pitches and are able to get the pitch booked, but football is played on grass. If you want to have a career in football, you need to understand how to play football on grass in football boots. Understanding offside and learning how to time your runs is an important part of football- organising the offside line for defenders and for goalkeepers commanding the box, knowing when to come for crosses, when to punch the ball, and when to catch. Some eleven-a-side games are played on Astro and you can develop some of these attributes, but playing on grass in football boots is a whole new experience for someone who has only played Astro football. Some players look amazing on Astro and then struggle on grass. Canaan was playing in football boots from six years old and is as comfortable in football boots as he is in trainers.

The next game in the Harrow League was against Concord Rangers, and the game was opposite the Queens Park Rangers Academy. Kevin was not going to be able to make this game as something had come up. The match would be coached by another coach. Concord Rangers were a team made up mostly of Asian players. The new coach was sticking to the same formation and players that started the last game against LNR. The match kicked off but something was different. From the first minute, Canaan was being man-marked and a player was tracking him everywhere he went. How did they know to man-mark my son? Did the coach know the

LNR coach? The player that marked Canaan was totally committed and sticking to Canaan. He did not allow Canaan to have any time on the ball and followed him everywhere. It was having an effect on Canaan's game. He couldn't get going into his flow. This player would not let him. We thought it would be a one-off when the player in the LNR match attempted to man-mark Canaan. I was happy, not with Canaan struggling, but because I thought this was excellent for his development. Now he was going to have to deal with being man-marked.

There are specific parts of Canaan's game that can only be developed in a competitive match environment. Competitive matches are important for youth development. There is only so much you can learn in training. I like to work on and highlight the areas that are difficult to develop in training. As Canaan got older, a lot of our discussions on his development changed. When he was younger, much of the conversation was based on him expressing himself and having fun enjoying his football. When Canaan started to get older, football got more serious and he knew he wanted to pursue football as a career. We would focus on areas of his game that could only be developed in competitive match environment conditions. The fact that Concord Rangers had man-marked Canaan was excellent for his learning and development. Canaan and I never spoke about what to do if he was man-marked. It was something that never came up, and coaches don't work on being man-marked in training as it's difficult to work on.

The match was a hard match for Canaan. He tried to move around and lose the marker but could not shake him. I knew after the match we would have a lot to talk about. It did not get any easier for Canaan because, in the second half of the match, Canaan took a hard, strong tackle. The tackle made him slam hard onto the ground. He was in a lot of pain and becoming stressed. I talked to him and tried to calm him down. The coach was rubbed Deep Freeze gel into his hip, and Canaan complained about the pain from his hip. The coach and I took him to the sideline, and the match continued on. It took about ten minutes for the pain to die down, and then Canaan was ready to go back on the pitch. Canaan managed to grab two assists and Regents Park ended up winning the game. However, Canaan was not happy with his performance and felt he never dealt with the man-marker.

'Don't worry, it's all part of your development and you will be better prepared for next time.'

The next game would be at Market Road in the Camden and Islington League. Canaan had been playing well in the Camden and Islington League. He was a threat at scoring goals. Regents Park was not getting the results they wanted. The next opponent was Unity. Unity was a good team. They were top of the league and I knew their coach. This game was a defining moment in mine and Kevin's relationship. Up to this point, Kevin was happy with Canaan. He was performing, scoring goals, and creating. In the Camden and Islington League, as it was seven-a-side, Kevin had been playing Canaan on the wing and allowing him to drift in from the wing, and that is where Canaan got most of his joy from. He had the freedom to cut inside and not stay out on the wing. Kevin had not expressed any problems with what Canaan was doing up to this point; he was being an absolute menace and scoring goals. During the match with Unity, Canaan was being a constant threat, as usual, and Kevin decided to tell Canaan to stay out wide and wait for the ball. It was not a tactical decision. He did not want him to cut inside anymore but to wait out on the wing for the ball. Canaan went from being a threat to a passenger waiting on the wing. One of Kevin's main players was not in the game anymore. Canaan was on the wing for nearly twenty minutes without touching the ball. Canaan started to get frustrated and decided to go in search of the ball; this annoyed Kevin and he subbed Canaan off the team.

Sometimes a coach will change formation or switch players about based on tactics or strategy and a player might have to be disciplined in a role for the team, but in this instance, the reason was because the coach said. It was not tactical, there was no strategy or plan behind the change, and this felt more like Kevin establishing his dominance over Canaan. Kevin knew Canaan had come from Isledon Wolves, a team that everyone knew for their pass and move and players interchanging. Canaan had been a part of that setup for the last three years. Kevin didn't care. His attitude was my way or the highway, do as I say, or you don't play. Kevin wanted Canaan to stay wide, get the ball, run down the wing, cross it in, and keep repeating the process. He wanted to strip Canaan down to a basic player, making him one-dimensional. A true coach does not want to develop one-dimensional players. They want players to achieve their full potential and become well-rounded players. Under Kevin, I felt Canaan would go backwards. Kevin wasn't a true coach. He was a volunteer, and I have spoken about the difference between coaches that believe in youth development passionately and volunteers who are helping out and giving back to the community. There is no substitute for a true coach. I had a conversation with Kevin about what happened in the match. Kevin was stubborn in his beliefs that he was right and I was wrong, and that Canaan needed to do what he said, or he would be benched. This is exactly what I am talking about when I say to be careful with who is responsible for your kid's development. Kevin works with under nines as well, which makes me shiver when I think about how their development was going.

I had to respect what Kevin wanted to do with his team and players, but I have a responsibility to Canaan's development. After I talked with Canaan, he decided to drop out of the Camden and Islington League and focus on the Harrow League. Canaan didn't have to be in both leagues if he didn't want to. It was his choice and, to be fair, he only wanted to do Harrow League in the first place. Kevin understood Canaan's decision and made it apparent there were no hard feelings. We respected each other's views. For Canaan, it was always about competing in the Harrow League and continuing his development as an attacking midfielder. Halfway through the season, he had fifteen goals and thirteen assists in the Harrow League. In the Camden and Islington League, his final tally was five goals and five assists. Canaan was going into every game expecting to score. Another game and he grabbed two more goals. At the end of the game, Canaan told me that his hip had felt sore. I told him we would monitor it to see if it kept giving him problems.

During a game against St Mary, Canaan grabbed another two goals and two assists. The match didn't have long to go and Kevin decided to make a change. He put Canaan up front. He said it would be better if he was a striker. Canaan spent the last ten minutes of the game with his back to the goal, waiting for the ball or chasing aimless long balls. This was frustrating watching from the sidelines. After the match ended, the coach of the St Mary's team asked Canaan if he was in an academy. Canaan said no, and the coach said he should be in one. It's nice to hear compliments like that; it helps us to stay focused and keep believing that what we are doing is correct in progressing Canaan's development. We hoped that Kevin playing Canaan up front was a one-off; besides, he had been playing attacking midfield for four months now and he was honing his skills: working on his movement and his runs, dealing with being man-marked, which seemed to be every match after the Concord Rangers match. But when it came to the next match, Canaan was starting up front as a striker. He spent most of the match isolated with his back to the goal. As I have said before, Canaan likes to create and be involved in linking the play. He is not an out-and-out goal scorer. Now, Kevin believed he was after working with Canaan for four months. He decided what he thought was best for Canaan after four months of him playing attacking midfield. It was confusing after how well Canaan was performing. When I asked Kevin for an explanation on his decision, he didn't have one; it was more about what he wanted to do, and he was more interested in explaining tactics and formations to me, not giving me a clear answer to my question. This was another volunteer focused on winning and not player development; to him, it did not matter what progress Canaan had made as an attacking midfielder for the last four months. All he cared about was winning the next match. As you can see, my priority was Canaan's development, and he was doing what he felt was best for the team.

During the match, Canaan spent most of his time waiting around for the ball. The team had lost its creative spark. He was the creative spark on the team, and this was the worst performance from Regents Park in the Harrow League I had seen up to this point. The through balls Canaan provided and his dribbling were all being missed. Regents Park looked out of balance, with no flow to the game. Canaan was the player who linked the play; without him in attacking midfield, the team looked disjointed. After the game, Kevin felt it was one of Regents Park's best performances and Canaan was excellent. I thought, *is this guy for real?* His players never thought that and the parents watching never thought that. I guess we must all be wrong. Canaan got two assists in the game, but they came from him dropping deep into his preferred position to get the ball. This was a frustrating time for Canaan. Here he was working tirelessly on his game as an attacking midfielder, wanting to get his game the best he could for when the team flew out to the Gothia Cup in a few months, and Kevin wanted to derail it by playing him as a striker. A combination of what happened in the Camden and Islington League and what was happening in the Harrow League made Canaan lose faith and trust in Kevin, and he knew he would not feel comfortable with him in another country. All I could do was explain to Kevin what I felt was best for Canaan's development, but it was Kevin's team and he made it clear that he could play his players where he wanted. All Canaan had asked for at the beginning of the season was to prove that he belonged in attacking midfield, and Canaan felt he had done that with flying colours, but now Kevin wanted to change it and didn't explain why.

After the match, Canaan was still complaining about the pain in his hip. We definitely felt it was from the Concord Rangers match, and it was not getting better. With all the issues with Kevin, we felt it was a good time to take a break from Regents Park and get Canaan's hip looked at in the hospital. Canaan had an X-ray done on his hip and the result was not good: he had a hairline fracture, and the doctor told him no football or any kind of sports for three to four weeks. Also, Canaan would need physio as part of the rehabilitation; he would be out for at least six weeks. He was not happy, but at least he didn't need surgery. It was a time for him to chill out and reflect on the season so far. Canaan's debut season had gone well, and he was happy. Kevin began sending out details for the trip to Sweden for the Gothia Cup tournament. Canaan didn't have enough trust in Kevin to be in another country with him and would feel uncomfortable in that situation. I explained to Kevin why Canaan would not be coming to the Gothia Cup: because he dropped him in the Camden and Islington League and to changed his position after four months in the same role when doing a fantastic job. Regents Park never lost with Canaan on the team playing attacking midfield.

Canaan was after a higher challenge. He wanted to move away from grassroots level and move into semi-pro and test himself at a higher level. Remember earlier when I said Canaan left Regents Park flying and top of the league? Well, when Canaan came back, the league was finished, and Regents Park had finished second. They had been knocked out of all the cups. Canaan came back in time to play an end of season cup tournament. There were three games. Kevin never played Canaan in the first game and they lost. He played him in the second game, where they drew, and also played him in the last game, and they won with Canaan grabbing the assist. This was a close tournament and went all the way to penalties. Regents Park was eventually knocked out on penalties. This was the first time Canaan had lost with Regents Park, and it was to penalties. Kevin thought Canaan had been immense. He said he was sharp, strong, and threading balls through the eye of a needle. Kevin felt Canaan didn't look like he had been away at all and was proud of him. I thanked him for his kind words and wished him all the best in the Gothia Cup. Kevin is an all-around nice guy. We had a difference of opinion when it came to Canaan. A couple of semi-pro clubs were interested in Canaan, and we looked forward to checking them out and to the new challenge that awaited.

CONCLUSION

As this book comes to a close, my plan is to enlighten as many parents as possible with my experiences at grassroots football. There is no real advice on youth football development for parents, on what is a good junior club from one that isn't, and good coaches from poor ones. All the advice seems to be is to get your kid into a pro academy as soon as possible and as you have seen through this book, I don't believe that is the best advice. I have spoken to parents and coaches and have tried to gain as many experiences as possible from different people as well as my own experiences. Some parents may see the sport their kid is doing as a hobby and not take that much of an interest in their development. The one thing that I notice with professional sports people is that there was someone that believed in them, whether that was one parent or both. David Beckham had his dad, Ted Beckham. Andy Murray had his mum, Judith Murray, and the list goes on. I wanted to give Canaan the best opportunity to have a career doing something he loves. Parents will do anything possible to get their kid into the best schools and universities because education is important, but what is more important is to encourage your kid to follow their dreams.

It's easy for parents to tell their kids to give up on their dreams because the dreams are not realistic, and they can actually become the person to destroy their dreams. Many actors, singers, sports people, and entrepreneurs had to ignore the people closest to them to pursue their dreams and goals, and if they had listened to those loved ones, they would have never achieved their dreams and had the impact on the planet that they have had and still do have. Parents will push their kids into a career like law or medicine because of the recognition and the money, not caring if their kid wants to do that as a career or not. Is education important? Yes, it is. Is chasing your dreams and being all you can be, making the biggest impact on this planet you can, important? Hell, yes! Becoming a footballer is a dream for Canaan. He wanted this dream since he was a kid, and we are still on this journey. To play professional football is the ultimate goal; it's the dream that Canaan is working towards. He is also pursuing other interests, and if that takes him into education or not, It's his life and he must live it, not me. Starting out on this journey with Canaan, there was no book like this. I do believe it would have been a great help. There are parents with young kids who want to get them into football and don't have a clue where to start. Because a junior club is local, it does not mean they are any good, but how would a mum know? I am hoping this book can help with advice and tips on finding a good junior club and coaches.

Dreams are fragile. We, as parents, have a responsibility to nurture them.

The biggest adventure you can take is to live the life of your dreams.

Oprah Winfrey

I would like to say a big thank you for buying a copy of my book and I am grateful for the support. Please leave a review; it means a lot to a new author like me.

Go here: https://eepurl.com/df_zbH

As a big 'Thank you' for buying my book, I would like to give you a free guide I created called Top Three Tips when choosing a Grassroots Football Coach.

If you are interested go to https://eepurl.com/df_zbH or scan the QR Code.

Also check out facebook.com/TechnicalStarsltd for help with anything grassroots.

Printed in Great Britain
by Amazon